Ocean Wisdom

Lessons from the Seashell Kingdom

By Michelle Hanson

Ocean Wisdom Press
34 Lynnhaven Road
Leominster, MA 01453
(978) 840-4357

The information in this book is for educational purposes. The author and publisher are in no way liable for misuse of the information.

Editor: Jenefer Angell, Passionfruit Editorial Services
Interior and exterior cover design: Michelle Hanson
CD Sound Engineer: Steve Wilson, Soaring Sounds Productions

ISBN-13: 978-0-9795041-0-5
ISBN-10:   0-9795041-0-4

It comes as no surprise that I am deeply grateful to all those who said "yes" and held the door open for me. Some not only held the door, but demonstrated remarkable patience waiting for me to walk through. These lessons from the seashell kingdom have taught me to be grateful as well to those who said "no." Although I was wounded at the time, had they not closed the door, I would have tried to fit in. I would never have considered forging a new trail and finding my truth.

As the Persian poet Rumi so inspiringly states in his poem, "The Guest House":

This being human is a guest house.
Every morning a new arrival.

A joy, a depression, a meanness,
some momentary awareness comes
as an unexpected visitor.

Welcome and entertain them all!
Even if they are a crowd of sorrows,
who violently sweep your house
empty of its furniture,
still, treat each guest honorably.
He may be clearing you out
for some new delight.

The dark thought, the shame, the malice,
meet them at the door laughing,
and invite them in.

Be grateful for whoever comes,
because each has been sent
as a guide from beyond.

Contents

Preface

This is the second book I have authored with seashells as my partners. The first, *Ocean Oracle,* is a collection of seashells and their associated meanings, learned though personal experience and a twenty-year history of shell readings with clients. In that book, readers are able to access messages from their inner selves by noticing an attraction to, or dislike of a shell.

This book has a different agenda. *Ocean Wisdom* is exactly that: wisdom from the seashells that provides new ways to think about aspects of our human journey. For instance, many of us have been taught to view survival, happiness, and generosity positively, and to think less warmly about selfishness or feeling flawed. The shells in this book illuminate that nothing we experience is good or bad in itself, but rather the key to fulfilling our life's purpose is balance. For example, while surviving is good, focusing too heavily on survival may compromise our ethics, or detour us from our path. The body survives, but at what cost to the spirit? Similarly, heartfelt generosity is a wonderful quality, but generosity borne from fear can be quite limiting. Conversely, if we are responsible for serving others, it's important to be selfish enough that we take time to recharge. What may feel like a flaw is in fact only something that makes us different, and it is our individual gifts that are the source of our contributions to the planet.

The shells offer guidance for searching our souls about our approach to everything, asking us to pause and evaluate our motivations, and helping us recognize whether we are working from fear or love. Fear masquerading as love prevents us from living in our truth. These shell lessons assist us in unmasking the imposter. They reveal hidden parts of ourselves that influence our lives whether we know it or not.

Acknowledgments

To my wonderful parents…your enduring love and support gift me with the safety to take risks.
To my loving husband, Don, my companion every step of the way…I cherish your partnership in my life's journey.

If it is true, "By their fruits you will know them," my deep appreciation extends to the following for their contributions to this succulent harvest:

To Anne Morrow Lindbergh for her trailblazing *Gift from the Sea*…thank you for paving the path;
To Casslyn Allen for initiating my journey with seashell energy…thank you for planting the seed;
To Neville Coleman for granting permission to share his powerful photography,
To Steve Wilson for listening to his guidance, creating marvels with sound,
To the many people who expanded my knowledge with insightful questions, and
To the many beings willing to add their voices to these pages…thank you all for your fortifying energy;
To Jenefer Angell for artfully improving this bounty…thank you for your tender pruning;
To my seashell partners…thank you for granting me stewardship of this garden of delights.

To one and all, my heartfelt gratitude!

Introduction: Challenging Comfort Zones

A mollusk is born with a perfectly fitted shell surrounding its body. With age, as the animal's body expands, discomfort is created in its now too-confining enclosure. New calcified material is added to accommodate its increased dimensions. Our own comfort zones likewise surround us like shells. They define our boundaries: "I will go this far, but no farther." Upon exposure to new thoughts and ideas, if we permit ourselves to grow, these comfort zones may stretch and expand to accommodate the new beings we become. When considering my relationship with seashells, my own comfort zone has mimicked the molluscan growth pattern. As my comfort zone expands, somewhere just short of the breaking point, I am granted time to acclimate in the new realm. Then I am stretched or pulled, and it is time to grow again.

After dabbling as a shell reader for twelve years, I was convinced of the shells' capacity to uplift and enlighten others, and felt secure in my hobby. Quite unexpectedly, my day job was abruptly terminated when the owner sold not only her business, but the territory as well. The employees were expressly forbidden to create their own similar business anywhere in the area. I was at a loss of what to do, when someone suggested advertising shell reading. I placed a small, experimental ad in a local metaphysical magazine. The results were far more than I bargained for. I was asked to write a column on shell divination—S-T-R-E-T-C-H—and to be interviewed on a radio show connected with their magazine. This led to TV appearances, newspaper interviews, and more publicity. Each step was another stretch of that comfort zone. I received telephone requests for shell readings, but was unable to comply because in order to do a reading I needed the person there to select their shells. This challenge stimulated me to find a way to export seashell divination for use anywhere in the world. My solution was to write a book—BIG S-T-R-E-T-C-H—with a companion deck of cards for performing readings. *Ocean Oracle: What Seashells Reveal about Our True Nature* was published by Beyond Words Publishing in 2004.

While still in the midst of writing *Ocean Oracle*, feeling secure in imparting the knowledge garnered from my shells, my comfort zone was stretched yet again. I received a call from a woman working with crystals who expressed an eagerness to add shells to her work. She wanted me to teach her how to work with shells as energy tools. Since I didn't work with shells that way, I readily admitted that I couldn't help her. Instead of accepting my position, she said, "That's OK. I'll wait. You'll figure it out and then you can teach me. And I think you will be teaching the teachers." I had no idea why she felt this, but I thanked her for her call intending to give it no more thought. That became increasingly difficult when, during the next two weeks, three additional crystal workers independently called with similar epiphanies. They too wanted to add shells to their work. My reply had not wavered from the one the first caller received, but these repetitive requests stirred my desire to have something to offer. With no idea how to proceed, I turned to meditation—S-T-R-E-T-C-H. I envisioned a blank screen and asked the shells to guide me. Suddenly, in my mind's eye, I saw Abalones and I wondered if they could help the crystal workers. What followed was a wonderful odyssey. Every new Abalone that entered my life pushed and pulled me to expanded awareness. Although I had never worked with energy before, the shells guided me to astonishing discoveries that I felt a responsibility to share.

The paramount factor in personal growth involves willingness to risk changing your comfort zone—STRETCHING. When new information is presented, it may be overlooked if we remain stuck in our current perceptions of the world. The shells offer a nurturing, safe place to discover our thoughts and beliefs and provide us with the opportunity to change anything that no longer serves us. To that end, this book concludes with a guided meditation encouraging a personal journey with these teachers. As you have seen, I have continued to stretch myself in order to reach the position to bring this information to you. May it assist you in growing into your truth.

Seashell Lessons

Consciously, we are aware of just a fraction of our entire being. We carry hidden thoughts, feelings, and beliefs that impact our lives even if we don't know it. As I discovered years ago, shells can be employed as tools to allow people to receive information from their subconscious minds, helping us to see these hidden beliefs, and granting us the opportunity to change whatever no longer serves us.

A fundamental premise of metaphysics teaches that, since everything is composed of energy, at this basic level we are all one. When we aid each other in becoming as true to ourselves as possible, we are all enhanced. If you will allow for the possibility that the beauty of shells extends beyond aesthetics, you will discover that Mother Nature communicates in a variety of ways. The shells work on an energetic level in concert with our Higher Self. No one knows us more intimately. It holds every joyous memory, every private wound we have buried or forgotten—every event that led to a belief about the world and ourselves. By guiding us to an attraction to specific shells, the Higher Self is able to deliver its message calling attention to hidden issues impacting our lives. Should you find yourself drawn to one type of shell in particular, please consider the possibility that your Higher Self is guiding you to work with this energy for a purpose.

The meanings connected to the shells derive from the name of the shell, the behavior of the mollusk (the animal who creates and inhabits the shell), or its interaction with man. I am delighted to have this opportunity to share a little of what the shells have taught me over the last twenty years of working with clients. In addition to molluscan shells, I have broadened the scope to include Starfish, Sea Urchins, and Sand Dollars.

Throughout *Ocean Wisdom*, you will notice the names of shells are capitalized only some of the time. The shell bears the same name as the animal who created it. A clam mollusk creates a Clam shell, and an abalone mollusk creates an Abalone shell. When you see the name capitalized, it refers to the shell. If it is not capitalized, it refers to the mollusk. This method of capitalization will help you distinguish whether I am referring to the animal or its shell, both of which are sources for the wisdom provided in this book. Starfish, Sea Urchins, and Sand Dollars are echinoderms, a term derived from the Greek word meaning "spiny skin." Since they are not mollusks, and these animals do not possess a separate shell, every reference to them is capitalized.

Survival

Starfish (back cover, photo 1)

Starfish represent survival against all the odds in a situation that disgusts you. This message is derived from two features of these animals:

First, when some species of Starfish are cut into sections, each piece containing a portion of the central core is capable of regenerating into a completely new Starfish. A few species can regenerate an entire Starfish from a single arm, producing several Starfish from one that is torn apart. Since Starfish dine upon oysters, they are the bane of oyster fishermen's existence. Some enterprising fishermen, in an effort to reduce the Starfish population in their area, hauled as many Starfish as they could aboard their fishing boat and chopped them into pieces. They then tossed these sections of Starfish back into the sea, unknowingly multiplying their problem.

Second, the Starfish has a very interesting digestive apparatus. It possesses two stomachs: the cardiac and the pyloric. When a Starfish has pried open an oyster's shell, it is faced with quite the dilemma. The reward for all of that exertion is an oyster that is too large to fit into its mouth. Undaunted, the Starfish relies upon its cardiac stomach, which is centrally located directly above its mouth. It pushes the cardiac stomach out through its mouth positioning it between the oyster's valves. Once the cardiac stomach has partially digested its prey, bite-sized morsels are passed inside the Starfish where the digestion is completed through the pyloric stomach. After absorbing the nutrients provided by this meal, the Starfish swallows its stomach back into its body. This technique of turning its stomach out of its body represents the situation that turns your stomach, or disgusts you. Starfish energy is designed to create a safe environment for you to confront hidden feelings of disgust. Rather than burying these offended feelings out of fear of acknowledging them, the Starfish are encouraging you to notice that this confrontation is necessary for your survival. When hiding or denying feelings, you are not living your truth. Whether you are deceiving yourself or others, you diminish yourself by expending a great deal of energy in order to keep these feelings buried, energy that could be employed in much more productive ways.

Conquering Victimization

Sand Dollar (*Mellita quinquiesperforata;* back cover, photo 7)

If you are feeling victimized in any way, Sand Dollar is here to help you understand that you create your life, and that everything that happens to you benefits you in some way even if you are not consciously aware of it. If a part of you feels "nothing ever works out for me" or "everyone abandons me," and indeed nothing *does* work out, or everyone *does* abandon you, then a hidden part of you gets the satisfaction of being right. In other words, what may appear to your conscious mind as failure is actually a success. Consciously, you may feel miserable, but deep inside those hidden parts are delighted when their beliefs are validated. Thus, you secretly understand that you have control over your life. While your conscious self may resist the idea that you deliberately create misery, understand that this is ultimately empowering. You are not a victim of circumstances and impositions by others. *You* create your life experiences; therefore you have control over what happens to you.

In that way, you are one with your Divine creator, which is why Sand Dollars are also reminders of the Divinity that dwells within us all. Many years ago, someone noticed the connection of the Sand Dollar to the life of Jesus. This was expressed in the anonymous poem, "The Legend of the Sand Dollar." (Please observe photo 7 as you contemplate the following.)

1

Written on this little seashell
There is a beautiful story
About the birth and death of Jesus
In all its wondrous glory

2

His wounds were five
And if you look closely here
You'll see four from the nails
One from a Roman's spear

3

There is also the Easter Lily
And in its center a star
One to remind us of his resurrection
The other of shepherds from afar

4

Now turn the dollar over
And here on the other side
A reminder of his nativity
The Poinsettia, sign of the Yuletide

5

Also during that season
We speak of Good Will and Peace
So if you break open the center
Five doves will you release

The five "doves" in the center are actually the Sand Dollar's teeth. Whatever your religious beliefs, whether you consider Jesus to be the Son of God, or a masterful teacher, Jesus represents the possibility of a connection to Divinity. If we recall that we are all composed of the same energy, then if the Sand Dollar contains evidence of God dwelling within it, it reflects the fact that God dwells within all of us.

Sand Dollar teaches that, far from being a victim, you are a Divine being, actively creating your life. You can conquer feelings of helplessness by recognizing that your beliefs determine your experience. Everything you say, every thought you think—can reshape your future. You have the power to create a Hell on Earth or paradise. Through awareness, the choice is yours.

Compassion

Razor Clam (*Ensis siliqua;* inside front cover, photo 10)

The streamlined shape of Razor Clam shells enables them to dig five to six feet underground, faster than a man with a shovel. Historically in England, razor clams were desirable for eating. Recognizing the futility of digging these clams out of their burrows, the English employed an alternative tactic. They sprinkled coarse salt on the ground over the clams' holes. This forced the clams to surface because their systems could not tolerate the bitter salt. Even though it placed them in danger, the overriding need to cleanse themselves of bitterness took priority.

As advocates of compassion, the razor clams teach us the importance of eliminating bitterness from our hearts. The salt on the surface of the clam's abode equates anger and resentment to the "salt" we rub into our own wounds. As Robin Casarjian states in *Houses of Healing*, anger allows us to create distance in relationships and prevents us from investigating the genuine feelings that dwell beneath. Whether in personal battles or massive conflicts, surface anger or resentment masks underlying fear or insecurities and separates us from claiming our true power. This leads to a condemnation of compassion as weakness, and a search for ways to obtain feelings of power and strength in an attempt to alleviate fear. Bitter feelings are used to justify violent responses. Just as Einstein asserted that a problem cannot be solved at the level at which it is created, violence inevitably reproduces violence. People become trapped in a vicious cycle based upon fear. How can we create a loving, peaceful world for our children using this recipe? The simple answer is that we can't.

We need a bridge to transport us from our world of fear to a new world vision of love. In her seminar entitled "Relating Beyond Conditions," Milagros Phillips explains that compassion and forgiveness are the components from which this bridge is assembled. Compassion enables us to treat an enemy with mercy and kindness, rather than as an opponent to conquer. For those who believe that compassion might become a source of weakness and lead to pain due to inappropriate sacrifices, the razor clams offer a new comprehension of the liberating strength inherent in compassion. Far from being a weakness, compassion will lead us to the true power we seek. Rooted in the truth of our love, no outside force can threaten us. By risking death to rid their systems of bitter poison, the razor clams are teaching us that danger is relative. Living with bitterness harbored inside us is even worse than death.

I can't improve upon this beautiful quote from Dr. Christiane Northrup: "Imagine all the angels and non-physical beings who are working on the other side to protect and uplift all of us. Know that they can only do their work in an atmosphere of compassion, not condemnation. The energy of condemnation will prevent them from connecting with the hearts of those who most need their inspiration and love."

Feeling Flawed
Delicate File Clam, Giant Lima (*Acesta phillipinensis;* inside front cover, photo 11)
For the lesson of the Delicate File Clam, sometimes known as the Giant Lima, we begin by examining the mollusk's anatomy and behavior. The file clam is a very poor swimmer unable to rely upon this skill to evade predatory fish. Fortunately, its body is equipped with a compensatory fringe of delicate tentacles peeking out from the edge of its shell. These tentacles break off easily and are quite sticky. They are the first bit of clam that enters the fish's mouth, and by wrapping around each other and sticking together, they effectively seal the unsuspecting fish's mouth shut. This buys the clam time to produce prodigious amounts of byssus threads, the same stringy filaments that mussels use to anchor themselves to wharves and rocks. While the fish struggles to unglue its mouth, the clam is able to bury itself in a quickly constructed nest.

In shell divination, the combined name and behavior of this clam suggests discomfort caused by the revelation of personal information so delicate that great effort would be made to keep someone's mouth shut rather than allow its disclosure. The clam's nesting behavior indicates that exposing this information would create such distress a person would have to hide away from the world in a "nest." What information could possibly be so damaging? Anything deemed to be a personal flaw, anything that makes us different—the fear of a person who believes that in order to be liked, he or she has to be like everyone else. Absorption in concerns about loss of acceptance dictates an inauthentic life lived in fear.

Thinking about our flaws, and the lesson from the file clam, I recalled a story circulating on the Internet a few years ago: "The Cracked Pot." In it, a water bearer has two pots, one perfect; the other with a large crack. Everyday, the water bearer walks to the stream and fills both pots with water. Upon his return, the perfect pot is full, but the cracked pot only has half its liquid contents. After a few years of this, the cracked pot says to the water bearer "I am so ashamed." When asked why, the pot explains that every day the water bearer works hard taking the two pots to the stream, but without fail, when they return, the cracked pot has lost half its water. The water bearer responds by asking the cracked pot to observe the ground when they visit the stream again. When they return the next day, the water bearer asks the pot how it feels. It comments that the flowers are beautiful, but laments that it is still only half full. The water bearer than asks if the pot noticed that the flowers were only on one side of the path—the cracked pot's side. The water bearer tells the cracked pot that every day on the walk back from the stream, the cracked pot waters seeds he has planted, and the water bearer is grateful the cracked pot is built precisely as it is. Thanks to this, they have beautiful bouquets for the Master's table.

What if the cracked pot had used all its resourcefulness and been able to prevent water from leaking out? The effort would take all its energy. Furthermore, there would have been no flowers adding color to the world. Like the pot, we often try to hide our cracks. Some people do it with drugs or alcohol, some fill their life with distractions to prevent others or themselves from noticing our self-described flaws, the things that make us different. However, hiding the crack is far more unhealthy than the crack could ever be. Moreover, as the cracked pot discovered, how do we know that the cracks we possess and judge as flaws are not the very thing that allows us to make our contribution to the planet and experience the joy of fully expressing ourselves?

Every transformation or invention comes from someone willing to be outside the box. If the Wright Brothers had listened to conventional wisdom, "If man were meant to fly, God would have given us wings" where would aviation be today? They listened to their hearts and knew flight was possible. They may have wished they could ignore their gut feelings and be accepted by others, but they chose instead to expose their cracks to the public. It's amazing to consider that following their hearts quite possibly required greater courage than confronting the actual danger of flying in the first airplane—it can be that challenging, but also, ultimately, that rewarding.

Instead of striving to be like everyone else by hiding the parts of you that feel different from others, cultivate those differences. Celebrate and appreciate your "cracks"and, through them, let the light of who you truly are shine out upon the world.

5

Feeling Special

Purpura Murex and Wide-Mouthed Purpura (*Bolinus brandaris, Purpura patula*; inside front cover, photos 12 and 13)

The word "purple" derives from man's interaction with shells and mollusks. The ancient Greeks called the territory near present-day Syria "Phoenicia," which means "land of the purple" in deference to the purple cloth they exported. During this period, there were not many methods for dying cloth. Someone discovered that the purpura murex secreted a clear fluid that when left out in the sun transitioned through various colors eventually arriving at what we now call purple. This fluid was capable of not only staining material, but more importantly, remaining permanently fixed in the cloth. The Phoenicians capitalized upon this discovery and introduced an entire industry of purple cloth production. Since each murex yielded only a few drops of punicin, the purple-producing chemical, it took thousands of murex to produce enough dye for one pound of cloth. This made the cloth prohibitively expensive. In fact, only royalty could afford it. To hasten the process, rather than waiting for the sun to perform the transformation, the mollusks were boiled. Amassing huge quantities of this material in enormous vats, caused a foul smell that was a cross between bromine gas and garlic. The dye vats had to be located down-wind from towns, and anyone wearing this cloth had to afford perfume to mask the odor. Here again, perfume was a luxury only royalty could afford. The color purple became symbolic of royalty, leading to the expression "born to the purple" to indicate someone of royal lineage.

In my work with clients, the Purpura Murex (also called the Purple Dye Murex) often gains attention by bothering people. If disliked, it reflects a desire to avoid anything that smacks of special treatment. While at first I thought this might be a tendency toward healthy humility, it was revealed that these clients so abhorred anything perceived as special, that they were deliberately limiting their own growth. These people fear that their special gifts will separate them from others and doom them to a lonely life. In order to avoid this isolation, they resist cultivating anything special within themselves. By abandoning their gifts, they hope to remain accepted by society, but the sacrifice prevents them from becoming all they can be. How many gifts are squandered because of these hidden concerns?

As we leave ancient Phoenicia and progress in time, we find other mollusks that contain similar dye-yielding chemicals. Today, in Latin America, the wide-mouthed purpura mollusks meet a kinder fate than those sacrificed in Phoenicia. Man has learned to milk their dye-producing glands by gently blowing inside their shell. This procedure permits the fluid to be obtained from the live mollusk, and allows the animal to continue producing future dye material. Both man and animal benefit as this technique manages to increase dye production while sparing the lives of the mollusks. Because of the foresight involved in this humane treatment by man, attraction to this shell indicates looking at the big picture, and working for the benefit of all.

If we consider that everything is composed of energy, and that we are therefore all one, then anything that enhances one individual enhances the whole. This is the new perspective taught by the Wide-Mouthed Purpura. In Dan Millman's book, *Way of the Peaceful Warrior*, Socrates tells his student "You've always tried to become superior in an ordinary realm. Now you're going to become ordinary in a superior realm." Living according to the Purple Dye Murex, someone might be concerned about trying to be special, or superior, in an ordinary realm. When it is rare or risky to step into our gifts, this could be viewed as a lonely path. Let's apply this to the life of Jesus. When his deeds were looked upon as miracles, and people placed him upon a pedestal—they made him special in their ordinary realm. However, he never encouraged that view. If anything, he insisted that anything he did they could do, and more. He was holding the vision of being ordinary in a special realm. The Wide-Mouthed Purpura echoes this approach, which encourages nurturing emotional and spiritual growth as a natural birthright for all. In such a society, the individuals would not be special, but the whole realm would be.

Faith
Tiger Cowrie (*Cypraea tigris*; back cover, photo 8 and 9)

If you have a dictionary handy, please check out the derivation of the word porcelain. You will discover that it refers to the vulva of a sow, a female pig. What, you may ask, does a pig have to do with porcelain? The answer requires a close inspection of the Cowrie shell. Turn to the back cover, and note that one outstanding quality of a Cowrie is its smooth finish. It looks and feels as though someone polished it. However, no human toil was involved. All mollusks possess soft, tender bodies (the word mollusk derives from the Latin word for soft). Since mollusks dwell inside their shells, the interior of their shells must avoid any scratches or cracks that could tear their body tissue. To prevent harm, some mollusks apply a smooth internal lining of mother-of-pearl, or nacre. To a sensitive mollusk, even a grain of sand can be enough of an irritant to cause the animal to wrap it in this nacre, as oysters do, which has the inadvertent result of creating pearls.

The cowrie mollusk prefers to wrap its body around the outside of its shell. Often, the shell is completely enveloped. Even with its flat design, to prevent potential body damage, the cowrie constantly reapplies a fresh coat of shell material to the entire exterior of its shell. This produces the gleaming finish and polished feel. The cowrie grows its shell in a fashion that is unique from other mollusks. As their bodies enlarge, and their shells become too confining, most mollusks simply add on newer, larger quarters to their existing shells. In many cases, the part of their body that manufactures the shell, the mantle, is only able to reach the new region of its shell. The shell territory from their younger years becomes too distant for repairs as it begins to fade and wear with time. In contrast the cowrie constantly adds new shell layers to its top surface, while it uses acid to eat away at the interior. This increases the internal surface area while allowing the mantle to repair any portion of the exterior shell. With this level of attention, the entire shell glistens to perfection. Even when fully grown, where other mollusks discontinue shell growth, the cowrie continues to add new layers of shell material throughout its life.

The other feature of all Cowrie shells is evident on the underside (photo 9). The aperture, or opening, is in the form of a toothy slit. This opening reminded ancient Europeans of the genital tract of their female pigs. Thus inspired, they called these shells *porcellana* shells meaning "little pig." When Marco Polo returned from China with never-before-seen glazed pottery, the polished surface reminded the Europeans of their porcellana shells, so they called the new pottery porcelain.

Apparently, this resemblance to the female reproductive tract occurred to man throughout history. In Pompeii, women connected Cowries with the womb and Goddess energy. They wore Cowries around their necks to prevent sterility. In Japan, the Tiger Cowrie is called the ko-yasu-gai shell. Roughly translated, this means the peaceful child shell. During labor, Japanese women would grip these Cowries in their hands, believing it would facilitate the childbirth. Should you think this connection to birth no longer applies, a Japanese exchange student shared the story that when she was pregnant in Japan, she visited a shrine and was given an obi (ceremonial sash) and this shell.

In shell divination, the Tiger Cowrie refers to someone possessing great faith in the birth of something new. This can relate to physical birth as discussed (Cowries would make a great asset on maternity wards), or to any creative birth process. We often hear comments about the "labor pains" involved, or someone's "baby" when referring to a project. As you broach any new creation in your life, consider the possibility that these Cowries may be there to soothe your fears, replacing them with the comfort of faith.

Hero's Journey
Scallop *(Pecten maximus*; inside front cover, photo 14)
If you have ever seen a Shell gasoline station, you are familiar with their Scallop logo. Have you ever wondered what a shell has to do with gasoline, and why the Scallop in particular?

Shell Oil traces its roots to Marcus Samuel who founded a small antique shop in London's east end in 1833. Among the more lucrative items in his store were shells imported from the Far East. In the 1800s, exotic shells from the orient appealed to Victorian decorative tastes. *The Shell Shop*, as he named it, eventually expanded to become a general importing-exporting company. Many years later, under his son's leadership, kerosene became a more valuable item than seashells. As the focus shifted to trading oil, in 1897 a separate company was formed for this called *The "Shell" Transport and Trading Company, Limited*. This eventually merged with Dutch petroleum interests becoming the company with which we are familiar today. The shell used in the gasoline logo is an acknowledgement of the company's humble origins.

As to the Scallop, centuries ago, Roman Catholics believed that pilgrimages on foot to the Holy Land would assist them in cleansing their sins. When the Holy Land was viewed as too dangerous a destination, the shrine to St. James the Apostle in Compostella, Spain became an alternative destination. Since St. James was a fisherman, it was common practice for pilgrims to obtain a local Scallop shell as a souvenir worn in one's hat brim. During the Holy Wars, crusaders would adorn themselves with Scallops they found in the lands where they fought. These became badges signifying they had participated in the wars in the Near East. Due to these long treks, both for the pilgrimages and the crusades, Scallops became symbolic of a journey.

The story of the Scallop does not end here. In the thirteenth century, courtesy of British Heraldry, many British families established coats of arms with symbols indicating their family's history. A brief glance at these reveals the tremendous popularity of Scallop-like motifs. This is the family's homage to their heroic ancestors who either made the pilgrimage or fought in the Holy Wars.

According to the Shell Oil Company's website, there is some evidence that the Shell emblem "may have been taken from the family coat of arms" of a Mr. Graham, who became one of the directors of the company. "The 'St. James's Shell' had been adopted by the Graham family after their ancestors made the pilgrimage to Santiago de Compostella in Spain." With nothing concrete, we are left to speculate whether Shell Oil was aware of the connection of Scallops to journeys. Regardless, what better symbol to represent a company whose products fuel our journeys!

Through British Heraldry, we have a connection of Scallops to heroism. The purest essence of knighthood was a noble person embodying all the finest attributes fighting for a cause, a hero who rescues others.

If we unite the original links of Scallops to journeying, with this later incarnation of representing a hero, we have the combination of a hero's journey. It requires great daring for each of us to make our own hero's journey. By summoning the courage to venture into unknown territory, we may overcome the limitations in our life. It is said that a journey of a thousand miles begins with a single step. Perhaps those huge Scallops hovering over us along the roadside can serve to prod us to take that first step on the road to a more meaningful life. They are a reminder of the bliss that awaits us on the journey.

Surrender
Great Green Turbo, Worm Shell, and Miller's Nutmeg (*Turbo marmoratus, Vermicularia spirata, Trigonostoma milleri*; inside front cover, photos 15, 16, and 17)

In the book *Seashells, Treasures from the Sea*, there is a wonderful discussion on Turban shells. One species, the Great Green Turbo, serves as currency for the Chambri tribe in New Guinea. These shells, which some texts claim can grow to be 8 inches, are exchanged for food and tobacco. To establish the shell's value, factors such as color, sheen, and size are taken into account. The shell is given a gender to add to its personality. What interested me is that its history and physical characteristics "combined to give each shell a value that had to be established anew every time it traded hands."

When I set off for college, I fantasized about the opportunity to start over. Nobody knew me—I could recreate myself! As it turns out, I remained pretty much the same shy person who graduated from high school. I held myself hostage to my history. Maybe nobody else knew me, but I knew me. The Green Turbo taught me that I did not need to be liberated from other people's thoughts about who I was, I needed to be liberated from my own. What if, like the Turbo, I could establish anew my own value in each moment? How many of my current behaviors are running on automatic pilot from years of ingrained beliefs about who I am? How can I really give myself the opportunity to grow if I am fettered to my former self? And, wouldn't it benefit all of us if we could grant that privilege to everyone with whom we relate? It becomes easy to move on and heal relationships, when we look upon each person as born anew in each moment. No former labels apply, no mistakes affect your present. When you are released from these, not just by others, but by severing your own shackles, you do "have it to do over."

This is living in the now: true freedom from past experiences, and freedom from future expectations. Miller's Nutmeg is the shell that relates to this idea. To understand why, we must investigate shell structure, in particular, the coiling pattern of univalves (mollusks with a single valve or shell). The vast majority of univalves produce tightly coiled shells. The seam between each coil, or whorl, is called the suture. The Miller's Nutmeg is very unusual because it separates the coils of its shell, but in a deliberately controlled growth pattern. The shell's structure is symmetrical, yet each whorl is separate, not sutured together. Thus, the Nutmeg is the embodiment of detaching from the past as well as the future. It is encouraging us to focus on the now.

Another unusual univalve, called a Worm Shell (no relation to worms), defies the regular pattern of other univalves. Close inspection reveals that the mollusk begins its life coiling its shell in the same tightly sutured fashion as other univalves, but at some point early in its growth it loses control of this process. The result is that the shell's structure appears to lack any guidance and grows in irregular random directions. The Worm Shell assists us in learning about the desire for imposing control. It attracts people who are experiencing situations that feel entirely out of their control. As their efforts prove futile, they resign themselves to surrender, and that state of mind permits spiritual connection and guidance.

If we combine the lessons of the Green Turbo (to grant ourselves permission to renew our value in each moment), the Miller's Nutmeg (to focus on the now), and the Worm Shell (to surrender control to Divine guidance), we have a blueprint to maximize our fulfillment moment by moment. The shells suggest that we surrender control, and surrender our history at each moment, so that Divine guidance will lead us to comprehend our real value as beings on this planet.

This surrender should not be interpreted as a sacrifice. Many people worry that they will have to deny their own desires if they are to live according to God's desire, but the shells are not proposing a battle between "my will" and "Thy will." These shells suggest that the fulfillment we seek comes from recognition that our Divinity knows our truth and holds the key to our happiness. If we align with "Thy will" by choice, human desire and Divine desire function as one. Without this connection, "my will" comes from the shallows of personality, and fulfilling them leads to short-lived satisfaction. Surrender is not about giving up your desires, nor will it deprive you of pleasure. It is about joining a wonderful silent partner who has been holding the knowledge of what would fill your soul with joy. By surrendering, you allow this silent voice to speak.

Love Lessons

The shells teach about love as an enormous wheel with an infinite number of spokes. Each spoke represents an approach to love: through the spoken word, through service, through spending quality time, through generosity and gift giving, through physical touch, through attention—or through any other path. Each spoke is of equal value. However, many of us select only one, considering the others to be inferior if we notice them at all. If quality time is what makes you feel loved, and your loved ones express love by giving gifts, you may not register the gift as love. If you require physical touch, then hearing "I love you" without being held doesn't affect you. How ironic to be surrounded by a feast of love, and yet if you don't recognize the other spokes on the wheel, you feel starved. Once you connect to the wheel at any spoke, allow yourself the freedom to explore the other spokes, until you can see them all. Love is the combination of all the spokes—the entire wheel. The whole is greater than the sum of its parts. Now let's look at some of these spokes in greater detail.

Love as Attention

Moon Snail (*Neverita duplicate*; inside front cover, photo 18)

Moon Snail tells us that things are being blown out of proportion. Moon snails absorb water into the exposed portion of their bodies, inflating themselves to three to four times larger than their normal size. Some species' shells become buried in the midst of their swollen flesh. The inflated animal must expel all this fluid before it can retreat back into the safety of its shell.

Moon Snail energy helps us reconsider reactions to a situation. Things may not be as disastrous as they seem. On a deeper level, the Higher Self guides us to Moon Snail to explore, as the saying goes, why someone might be invested in "making mountains out of molehills." If someone constantly views experiences as catastrophes, Moon Snail helps reveal the hidden benefits that person might gain from this perspective. Typically, the sympathy and attention these circumstances bring is unconsciously interpreted as love, which in turn creates a need to maintain a steady supply of catastrophes. People attracted to Moon Snail need the mountains because they believe that molehills won't get them the attention they crave. And if everyone has a mountain to deal with, then they need to make their mountain even higher: "If you think that person's experience was bad, wait until you hear what happened to me." Like a "problem child," they have learned that they have to make noise to be noticed. Later in life, the "noise" becomes translated into calamities, physical illness, and so forth. Notice how transforming molehills into mountains requires harming the self in some way.

If you have chosen the Moon Snail, your hidden beliefs must be confronted before they can heal. Allow Moon Snail to work with you to accomplish this. You may require attention to feel loved, but physical, financial, or emotional miseries are not the only ways to gain attention. Since Moon Snail is simply about inflating your experiences, it is also possible to use Moon Snail energy to inflate the positive events in your life.

I learned this lesson from Pat Prevost, a wonderful teacher whose spiritual name happens to be Little Moon Snail. My husband discovered her by searching under "seashell oracle" on the Internet. This led to a three-hour telephone conversation during which she told me that her favorite shell was the Moon Snail. When I related the message that this shell had revealed to me, she admitted that she had experienced life-long disasters. As we spoke, she had an epiphany. Acknowledging her need for attention, she realized that she could achieve the same results by expanding upon joyful experiences. She became excited as she connected this revelation to a recent conversation with a friend. Her friend declared: "You can take any light and make it brighter." I can not think of a more eloquent way to describe this alternative application of Moon Snail energy.

Are you familiar with the expression "misery loves company"? Subscribing to this philosophy uses misery as a socializing tool. When hurting, many people congregate with others who are in pain. If a person achieves a degree of happiness, she may find herself alone until the next calamity. Then she is welcomed back into the group as they dispense consolation and understanding. Sometimes those who are content don't receive attention from others, not because they are not loved, but because they are perceived as not needing it. Somehow, we have learned that the ones who need attention are those who are suffering, which causes many people to reinforce their own suffering.

From that perspective, allowing oneself to be happy may jeopardize opportunities to feel love from others. For those who require external validation, seeking happiness could become counter-productive. Moon Snail teaches that we can shift this paradigm. Why can't *joy* love company? Why can't *love* love company? What if we paid attention to the well-behaved children as well as the rambunctious, encouraging their happiness as a way to receive loving attention? Wouldn't it be wonderful if we could show love to everyone regardless of one's state of happiness?

As I was writing about this lesson from Moon Snail, I experienced a remarkable demonstration of this exact thing. A girlfriend of mine called and I took the call because I could tell she had a problem. In the midst of our pleasant conversation, she suddenly commented that she felt she had to be hurting to get time with me. I am ashamed to admit that she was right: Unknowingly, I had set up a screening process, deciding who "deserved" my attention based on their degree of need. My friends and I were mutually supporting what Moon Snail teaches: the worse the misery, the more attention people receive. Once I became aware of this, I set out to apply Moon Snail energy by making the light brighter. Whenever someone called with good news, I shared that with others. I was amazed to see how quickly the process worked in reverse. If I paid attention to good news, my friends felt encouraged to share the magical events in their lives. I am no different. I found myself involved in a whirlwind of fantastic occurrences created from a desire to share the wonders of the Universe with those I love. Now the comments became, "If you think that is amazing, listen to this."

When we are willing to pay attention to the marvelous and magical events in each other's lives, when the happy person isn't sentenced to the end of the "deserving love" line, we create a safe environment to increase the amount of joy in the world. Ultimately, inflating joy—isn't that a wonderful testimony to the lesson of Moon Snail?

How perfect that this new perspective on Moon Snail would come from a conversation with someone named Little Moon Snail. Since she is my partner in discovering this information you are reading today, I thought you would like to "meet" her. I wrote to Pat to ask her how she came to be called Little Moon Snail. Her story is a perfect example of how listening deeply to yourself allows the messages of life to reveal themselves and lead you to joy:

Ever since I was a little one, I have always been drawn to shells. I was so taken by the spiral of the shell and the fact that someone lived inside of it, never mind also built it. I saw how other creatures would find empty ones and would call them their homes as well...how what we leave behind can sometimes be so significant to another's life.

All through my life, wherever in nature I went, I could always spot the snails whether aquatic or land ones. I was surprised at the different sizes, colors, and bravado of each type and would pick up an empty one to cherish for a while.

It seems in reflection that, where in my life I had the most growth in personal challenges, there were large populations of moon snails. But at the time I did not connect this fact. Only in Shelley's oracle did I begin to realize what they had meant in my life and the signposts they had been for me growing into my light.

Just a few years ago I was drawn heavily back into the shells as I began creating unique sets of shells as oracles for people. Once again the snails and I fell in love. Each time that I touched them I knew that they were my shell totem. There grew a peace that came with touching them and it echoed inside enough to hear someone call my name....Little Moon Snail.

It made sense because over the past years I had been heavily working with the lunar cycle and its Goddesses to help the people and the animals I work with to understand their connections to the moon—the earth's most intimate satellite. Each time I observed a lunar phase ceremony I could hear my native name inside. Then at a sacred site, I attended a summer solstice ceremony conducted by a pipe carrier medicine woman whom I have come to know. I thought to ask the ancestors and nature spirits there for a sign to confirm that this is my name.

I worked with turkey vulture medicine (shape-shifting medicine) and at the ceremony as I asked for a sign, a turkey vulture flew low over the circle of women gathered. I knew it was Eli my vulture, who was with me again in spirit through the body of this vulture celebrating my name above. And so we got to yell out our names to the four directions on the medicine wheel to let the ancestors know that we were there, and to let them know how they would know us in future ceremonies. It just felt so right as if I had been there for always and I was truly Little Moon Snail.

Then Shelley found me and she told me about the moon snail in her oracle. There displayed were the challenges of my life's work. I had worked so hard to transform myself by refusing to follow the path that those before me had laid down in their suffering. Not only was the spiral in the shell, the Goddess spiral, and the sacred geometry of the shell's form an inspiration of life that computer programs cannot reproduce, but it had new meanings for me. It served as confirmation of the work I had done to arrive in the place of peace and healing I am in now.

Aho! I AM Little Moon Snail

Love as Quality Time
Shuttlecock Volva (*Volva volva*; inside front cover, photo 19)
In seashell divination, some meanings derive from the name and appearance of the shell, such as is the case for the Shuttelcock Volva. Its lesson is about being pulled in two directions, caught in a triangular relationship. In the game of Badminton, the shuttlecock is batted back and forth across a net. It no sooner arrives on one side, then it is hit back to the other. When this movement in two directions occurs in relationships, it can be very uncomfortable. It may require a difficult choice as to where, or with whom, one's support, attention, or love will dwell. The "where" may take the form of one person choosing between another and other desires such as work, hobbies, and friends. "With whom" may express itself as a triangular relationship with two people battling for the attention of the third. Triangles may take the form of competition in other arenas, such as at work, or with friends, where there is an opportunity to be chosen over a coworker for some project, or to be singled out as someone's best friend. People selecting this shell may be on any point of the triangle. They may experience being the one pulled in two directions, demonstrating their love for the others involved, but most often they are the one needing to be chosen, seeking proof that they are loved. Action (in the form of being chosen) speaks louder than words.

Such people equate love with time together. In fact, they may distrust the words "I love you" if uttered by someone who is never around. An underlying need of "proof" of someone's affection may cause them to become constantly involved in triangles as a pattern in life. Each triangle provides them with another opportunity to be the one chosen, to have someone's actions say "I choose to be with you over any other alternative." When this occurs, they have gained what they most highly prize: quality time, a demonstration of love mere words could not convey.

Love as Generosity
Mussel (*Mytilus edulis*; inside front cover, photo 20)
Mussels secrete a liquid material that quickly hardens into stringy filamentous threads called byssus. These threads serve as anchors to wharves and rocks preventing the mussels from becoming dislodged and damaged by the tides. When a mussel does relocate, the journey begins by loosening a few threads and repositioning them. Once these are secure, they loosen a few more old ones to add to the new site. This process continues until the animal is fully relocated. By this means, they are capable of climbing up wooden piers, or to more desirable rocky locales. With these stable foundations, they are able to survive the pounding waves.

Since, literally, there are strings attached to their every move, attraction to the Mussel shell may indicate a person who believes nothing is offered without something being expected in return. Such people doubt that anything comes from the goodness of the heart. They respond to generosity with suspicion, and wonder what people want from them in exchange? If your Higher Self guides you to Mussels, let yourself receive the awareness that you believe there is a hidden agenda behind people's motives.

Often, what we see in others is a reflection of what we deny within ourselves. Although people attracted to Mussel shells may view others' generosity with suspicion, they are commonly quite generous themselves. If this is the case, these good deeds might benefit from investigation. Are they performed as insurance against the time assistance may be necessary? If someone carries a hidden belief that she can't rely upon the kindness of others, she may find herself driven to perform all kinds of deeds for others, unaware of her motivation. She is banking upon their indebtedness. Should the time come when she requires aide, they will owe her. Ironically, a person living this way is the one operating with strings attached. She is giving out of fear, not love.

Mussels are here to help reexamine views of life. Are you performing generous acts as insurance? If so, can you alter this perception to liberate yourself to be inspired towards heartfelt generosity, but to recognize generosity that comes from a sense of fear? When your Higher Self guides you to Mussel shells, it is attempting to reveal hidden beliefs that impact your life: What acts do you suspect engender indebtedness? Exposing these beliefs allows you the opportunity, if you desire, to change whatever no longer serves you.

Love as Selfishness
Venus Comb Murex (*Murex pecten*; inside front cover, photo 21)
In the conventions of seashell nomenclature, the first person who finds a shell is entitled to name it. Although the scientific name must comprise the Latin genus and species, the common name can be anything. In the case of the Venus Comb Murex, the person who discovered this shell may have imagined a mermaid combing through her tresses with the protruding spines. Just as primping with a comb symbolizes absorption with the self, this shell indicates a desire to take care of, and pursue, one's own needs. It encourages healthy self-centeredness, self-love, focusing on one's needs, and discovering and living one's truth.

Take a look at the photo and see how you react. If it appeals to you, then you are someone willing to focus upon your own needs. However, many people are frightened by its appearance, seeing a skeletal image instead of the visions of mermaids combing their hair. Disliking this shell may indicate someone who is focused upon everyone else's needs while paying no attention to his own. For this person, the word "selfish" has negative connotations. Disliking this shell reveals an uneasy feeling that one may end up drained by those who constantly require attention. It's important not to get so depleted attending to others that a person has no energy available for himself.

The title of this lesson, Love as Selfishness, makes some people uncomfortable. They have been taught that a loving person is selfless. Consequently, they become willing to take care of everyone else's needs while their own needs are unmet. If a person operates this way, eventually there comes a time when there is something else he would rather do, but he can't let himself for fear it will be perceived as selfishness. Now, because of the sacrifices he must make, he is faced with having to take care of someone else while he is carrying the emotional energy of anger, depression, or resentment. He can't even express these sentiments forcing a smile lest his feelings betray him. Choosing to suppress his needs does not benefit him, but ironically, taking care of others while harboring anger or depression does not benefit them. On the other hand, if he allows himself to be one of the people he is willing to take care of, each little thing he does for himself will create increased levels of happiness. Then when he chooses to take care of others, they are around a person who is radiating positive energy and everyone benefits.

Beyond this, let's examine the original goal: He was determined to be unselfish so he would be loved. However, if he has never focused upon his own desires and expressed them, then when someone does tell him they love him, somewhere in the back of his head he may hear a voice saying "How can you love me? You don't even know me." In fact, if he has not allowed himself permission for self-exploration, he may not even know who he is himself. This love is not fulfilling because the other person is only loving a projected image, an illusion created from his fear of risking the perceived selfish act of focusing on his own desires and needs. Recall the famous words: "to thine own self be true." When he allows himself time to discover his truth and live in that truth, then when he hears someone say "I love you" they are responding to his authentic self. With this new "selfish" way of loving there is no doubt they are talking about the "real him", and he will feel that love all the way to his soul.

One word of caution: When taking care of other peoples' needs becomes limiting, pursuing self-love may require saying "no." For many, the act of saying "no" is difficult—it is the very definition of selfishness. People who can't express this sometimes become physically incapacitated, as it gives a person permission not to have to take care of anyone. Saying "no" and being physically incapacitated accomplish the same goal. For those ingrained in the fear of being perceived as selfish, saying "no" can be the more difficult option. It is my hope that with this new understanding of the benefits of selfishness, the word "no" will become easier to embrace.

Perceptions of Beauty
Land Snail, Janthina, and Harp Shell (*Placostylus, Janthina janthina, Harpa ventricosa;*
inside front cover, photos 22, 23, and 24)
As we know, beauty is subjective. I would like to alter your perception of beauty by looking at the world through the eyes of a mollusk.

When I mention the word snail, what do you envision? Most people associate snails with a "slimy" quality. Snails are mollusks, a Latin word meaning soft-bodied. As their tender bodies glide along the rough terrain, land snails use mucus to lubricate their path. The mucus is so effective at protecting mollusks that they have been observed crawling over upended razor blades unharmed. When we encounter "razor blades" placed in our path, many of us halt in our tracks or take a detour around them. Because of mucus, the snail continues on its path uninterrupted. It doesn't perceive the razor as an obstacle, much less a source of danger. And, for the snail, it proves to be neither. This offers a lesson in the power of belief. There are those among us capable of lying down on a bed of nails and arising unharmed, due to their spiritual "mucus." We create our experiences based upon our beliefs.

Let's leave the land snails and look at other specialists employing mucus in magical ways: the janthina and the harp snails. The purple-hued Janthina shell (photo 23) is as light as air. In seashell divination, attraction to this shell indicates a desire to cling to a fantasy world. To understand why, we must explore the life of the janthina, also known as the Purple Sailor, which lives far from shore on the ocean's surface. This may not seem like much of an accomplishment until you stop to consider that this animal can't swim. How is it able to live on the surface of the ocean? It uses mucus to cement air bubbles together and constructs a raft. The janthina spends its entire life floating on its raft, hence the moniker "Purple Sailor." If it becomes dislodged from the raft, it drowns. Its survival depends upon clinging to the bubbles, just as we may live in our own "bubble" fantasy world. In addition, the janthina snail is blind. So it can be challenging for people attracted to this shell to see the fantasy they're living in.

My favorite illustration of this shell's energy speaking to someone happened during a pre-interview conducted at my home for a local TV talk show. With almost 500 shells displayed in my cabinets, the host was drawn only to the Janthina. She was not expecting a reading, but her curiosity prompted her to ask about this shell. The first thing I told her was that the animal that made it can't swim, to which she replied, "I can't swim." I immediately followed up with telling her it is also blind. Her response: "I am blind in one eye." I felt as if I were speaking to a human janthina. The odds of her selecting the one shell whose mollusk shared, and thereby revealed, two hidden traits she possessed captivated her attention. As she later told her audience, this "made a believer" out of her. She was open to listening to the message connected to the shell. I discussed the possibility that she might be living in a fantasy, which led to her selecting more shells to elaborate on the details. To her credit, when I appeared on her show, she recounted this entire story to her audience even admitting to the fact that the Janthina brought awareness that she had been living in denial. She was so blind to her fantasy, no person could succeed in bringing this to her attention. It took an unexpected encounter with a shell to break through the bubble she had created.

Once I discovered how rooted my clients can be in their denial, using the *Ocean Oracle* card deck provided an unexpected bonus. If the Janthina appears in a reading, I use a different strategy. Since the meaning of each shell appears on the back of the cards, rather than telling them about the Janthina's message of denial, I turn over the card and have them read the information themselves. This delivers more of an impact than anything I could say. More than once, after reading about the Janthina, my clients have admitted that their friends have tried to tell them something but they refused to see. It is stunning to witness how this little shell reaches through walls that no humans could penetrate.

The harp snail (number 24) has developed its own wonderful employment of mucus. The harp has the ability to detach a portion of its foot. This is a small sacrifice as the foot will regenerate. It uses this ability when pursued by a predator, such as a crab. Since the crab is seeking to dine on the harp, by shedding a portion of its foot to preoccupy the crab, the harp could get away. Instead, while the crab is enjoying its morsel, the harp secretes mucus, mixing it with sand, and coats the crab. The unsuspecting crab becomes immobilized, and the harp eats it. Willing to make a small sacrifice, the harp receives a big reward. It completely turns the tables, enabling the intended victim to be the victor. In shell divination, attraction to the Harp is about making present sacrifices for future rewards. You can completely turn the tables from the status of victim to victor.

As you explore the world around you, I hope these examples encourage you to look at the world through new eyes. If mollusks' eyes could alter the way you perceive mucus, what might insects' eyes, or birds' or other animals' eyes lead you to discover? What about flowers or trees? Consider the wind, or the ocean. (See page 37.) Imagine looking at the world from these alternative perspectives, and see what beauty is right before your eyes.

Judgment
Textile Cone Shell, Geography Cone Shell, and Magus Cone (*Conus textile, Conus geographus, Conus magus*; inside front cover, photos 25, 26, and 27)

Cone shells' interactions with man present a wonderful opportunity to look at the issue of judgement. Cone mollusks are unique in the anatomical apparatus they possess for feeding. They are carnivores, but unlike other carnivore mollusks, cones use poison to paralyze their prey. A gland in their head serves as the reservoir for the poison. Their teeth are shaped like tiny harpoons connected to this gland through a tube. The poison is similar to snake venom, and upon injection the prey experiences an inability to mount any coordinated response. This is rapidly followed by a systematic shut down of each internal organ. Through this mechanism, a snail can eat a fish. Although all cones contain this harpoon delivery system, not all poisons are equally toxic. Some cones only eat tubeworms, and they are far less dangerous to man than those that eat fish. A few cones, such as the textile and geography cones (photos 25 and 26) carry a more potent and dangerous dosage.

Although geography cones are among the deadliest, scientists discovered that by altering their paralyzing venom just a little, it serves medicinally for those patients suffering from tremors. Apparently, the paralyzing action of the venom counteracts the shaking. Here is where the lesson of judgment can be applied: had an early judgment been made to rid the planet of these dangerous cone mollusks, we would have eliminated access to a powerful medicine we are only just beginning to recognize. And geography cones are not the only cone species involved. Over the years, reports have increased on how cone venoms, termed conotoxins, are used medicinally. In January 2004, following clinical trials, scientists announced that a protein found in the poison cocktail from the magus cone is a very effective painkiller that gives relief to cancer and AIDS patients who can no longer take morphine. In 2005, *Newsweek* reported that a drug mimicking another conotoxin provided relief for patients suffering from chronic back pain. The research continues as scientists await the next medical conotoxin breakthrough.

The lesson of the Cone shell arose in my life at the start of my career as a shell reader. While seashell reading was merely a hobby, I was once a nutritionist working for a weight loss center. The owner was absentee, and due to low revenues she had cut my hours back to four per week. I had grown close to my clients, and did not want to cancel our appointments. My solution, which my manager did not seem to mind, was to put in a full week and simply fill out my time card for four hours. This did not cheat the owner, and I was able to continue working with my clients. Problem solved, until suddenly my world came crashing down. Overnight, the owner sold the business and her territory as well. The employees received no advance notice, and were expressly forbidden to open a similar business anywhere within this vast territory. To me, the owner's actions were a poison destroying my life. I was paralyzed, completely at a loss about what to do. In the midst of my panic, someone suggested advertising my shell readings. I placed a small ad in a metaphysical journal, and was immediately asked to write an article. This led to a request for a radio interview and opportunities to work at psychic fairs. To prevent damaging my shells, I photographed them and found that photographic images worked just as well. Later on, this knowledge gave me the confidence to export the shells through a deck of cards with a companion book.

In hindsight, when the owner cut back my hours, I continued working anyway. It required a clean sweep, selling her territory, to completely remove any possibility for me to continue working as a nutritionist. (Could this clean sweep be the "crowd of sorrows who violently sweep your house empty of its furniture" as described in Rumi's poem, "The Guest House"? See the dedication.) As Rumi observes, "He may be clearing you out for some new delight." What I judged to be lethal proved to be medicinal. Eradicating my current life had forced me to redirect my career and discover a new passion far more fulfilling than my life as a nutritionist. My quiet little shell-reading hobby finally became public knowledge. The "poison" might end an existing way of life, but also pave the path to something better.

Questions to Consider

The meanings connected to the following shells do not derive from a scientific source. They are not based upon the behavior of the animals, nor are they due to the interaction with humans. They come from intuition that challenges us to search our souls. They explore our beliefs regarding the value of struggle, or pride, the need to be right, or even confronting our destiny. Working with these shells can lead to dramatic revelations that can prove transformational.

Struggle

Tropidophora Land Snail (*Tropidophora deliciosa*; inside front cover, photo 28)
Attraction to this shell indicates a belief that life is a constant struggle, with nothing handed over easily. This person has learned value comes from struggle and is not interested in anything that comes too easily. Ascending the mountain, we may be flown up by helicopter or we may claw our way through the back trails on foot. This person would not appreciate the view unless arriving scraped and bruised from the arduous climb.

Let's apply this to relationships. Imagine a woman attracted to the Tropidophora shell entering a club. A man approaches her who is immediately smitten, and begins extolling her virtues. Another man won't give her the time of day. Since she has to earn the second man's attention, this challenge increases its value. When the Tropidophora is involved, it is time to ask yourself these questions: Can I value something if it is easy? Would I be happy with someone instantly attracted to me? Would I value an item given to me if I didn't have to work for it? Can I accept something [an object, a job, love] if it is given freely, or must I struggle to feel I earned it? If you are willing, the view from the top can be just as lovely, no matter what route you took to arrive there.

Pride

Sea Biscuit (*Clypeaster rosaceus;* inside front cover, photo 29)
Sea Biscuit teaches about pride. Pride is all about external validation: relying upon other peoples' feedback to determine self-worth. A proud person carefully orchestrates all actions to elicit proof that she deserves love and avoids doing or saying anything that might take the admiration away. Such a person may succeed in maintaining a balance on someone's pedestal, but at the price of self-respect. Maintaining the halo becomes challenging when she denies her truth to keep from falling off her precarious perch. Someone once observed that a halo only has to slip a few inches to become a noose. As the life is squeezed out of her, anger arises at the one who placed her on that pedestal. Soon enough, the finger of blame comes full circle and points back at the self, and in that clarity she wonders how she could have given another that much power over her.

With Sea Biscuit, the important question becomes "Do I care more what you think of me, or what I think of me?" I can get you to love me, but at what cost? Is it worth it, if I lose my identity in the process? If you find that craving this external validation no longer serves you, adopt the motto: Other people's opinions of me are none of my business.

Vindication

Fossil Cephalopod (inside front cover, photo 30)
With this shell, the need to be right supersedes all else. When something expected manifests, whether positive or negative, it is subconsciously received with equal joy.

When combined with any other belief, this need to be right is very powerful. When someone believes he is unlucky in love, then it benefits him to encounter unhealthy relationships rather than wonderful partners because this makes him right. No matter how much he may consciously suffer from heartbreak, the hidden part of him that needs to be right gets to celebrate. If he believes people are dishonest, then it benefits him to encounter liars rather than those who tell the truth because this makes him right. No matter how much he may suffer consciously, the hidden part of him that needs to be right gets validated.

When it becomes more important to be right than to be happy, then this need is limiting your life. There are two possible solutions: allow yourself to be wrong or change the thing you are right about. If, as in the above example, you believe you are unlucky in love, you can change the thing you are right about by choosing to believe you will find the perfect partner, and through this create circumstances to be right about that belief. Alternatively, you can allow yourself to be wrong about your belief. Let's say you encounter a wonderful partner who loves you. This would disprove your original belief that you are unlucky in love. If you can accept being wrong, then this can continue to be a very nurturing relationship. However, if you can't accept being wrong, the relationship will no longer hold promise, making you right, but unlucky. The questions are: What beliefs do I hold that may be limiting my quality of life? How important is it for me to be right about these beliefs? Is it OK for me to be wrong?

People attracted to this fossil may have developed a need at a young age to be the one that others can come to for advice. Their self-esteem increases every time someone praises their good advice. The desire to be right about everything may lead to constant devotion to study so that all questions can be answered. Because they invest so much in having all of the answers, they may find themselves learning things that are not of personal interest. Instead of learning out of passion, they learn out of fear. Their concern: What if I don't have the answers? They won't like me anymore. For this reason, they have a lot invested in learning everything they can in preparation for the day someone asks about that subject. Disliking this fossil reveals the limitations this habit places upon one's time. The inner self is suggesting that the need to be right has become a trap that is diminishing the quality of life. There are only so many hours in the day, and they are better devoted to pursuing subjects that hold personal appeal. In this case, the questions to ask are: Is it OK if I don't know the answers? Will they think less of me if I admit I don't know? What have I studied out of fear that I can now release? What would I like to pursue that I have not had time for?

Many of you reading this book have an interest in inner knowledge. This fossil addresses this as well. If this shell is disliked, it may indicate a past experience when a person senses something terrible and would prefer to be wrong than have these thoughts confirmed. Such people may actually shun their intuitive feelings. Unlike the people attracted to the shell who must avoid being wrong, these people are trying to avoid knowledge that can carry pain. For example, suppose you knew intuitively that your best friend's husband was cheating on her. You would wish with all your heart that you were wrong. You have no desire to be proven right. The pain of this could cause you to turn off your intuition rather than know such things. People actively pursuing a spiritual path need to resolve this feeling if they are to allow their intuition to function at full capacity. The desire to know the "good" events and not know the "bad" ones will limit the ability to know anything. Intuition is all or nothing. You don't have the luxury to only know some things and not others. Fortunately, as you will see later in this book, at the highest source, there is no judgment; everything that happens is for our highest good. But for now, just know that this fossil wants to make you aware of this possible blockage in your quest for spiritual knowledge.

Destiny
Long-Spined Star Shell (*Astraea phoebia*; inside front cover, photo 31)
People attracted to this shell may feel eager to fulfill a life mission without knowing that they subconsciously perceive dangers along the path that cause them to sabotage their plans. Considering the subject of fulfilling one's destiny leads us to its most famous role model: Jesus, whose destiny was crucifixion. Society no longer literally nails people to a cross, but still inflicts pain with mental torment or taunting, jeering, criticizing, or ostracism—experiences so unpleasant that people may avoid their destinies, subconsciously afraid of this modern "crucifixion." If you carry the hidden belief that your

destiny may involve torture, every obstacle to stepping into one's life purpose delays the crucifixion that awaits you. Once you understand that you created these obstacles yourself as a form of protection, you have options. Just as Jesus was "the last sacrifice," if we choose, we can adjust our beliefs so that we see a way to fulfill a delicious destiny without harm to ourselves. The question here: Do I believe that my choice to fulfill my destiny would require my crucifixion? If you remove the possibility of torture, you no longer need to avoid your mission, and you will find the obstacles fall away making the steps on your path easier to walk.

Consider also that for some the degree of suffering is directly proportional to the value of the destiny. For these people, the crucifixion is beneficial as a confirmation that one's destiny is more noble. The question then becomes: Can my destiny hold great purpose if I don't have to suffer to fulfill it?

Trust

Helmet Conch (*Cassis tuberosa*; front cover, photo 34)

If mankind's spiritual ideal is to achieve a place of compassion and unconditional love, all we need do is regard our domestic pets to see they already possess these qualities. If you are willing to concede that these animals are pretty high up on the evolutionary ladder, what about a snail? Surely man is more highly evolved than a snail. Before deciding on an answer, consider the story of the Helmet Conch, a member of the snail family.

Helmet Conchs, large shells that grow to be 8 to 12 inches long, were so named because their appearance resembles helmets worn by ancient warriors. For this reason, in divination, Helmet Conchs represented someone willing to fight for you.

In *Shells Alive,* Neville Coleman, the Australian biologist, writes in great detail about his encounter with a group of Helmet Conch snails. During his routine recording of underwater functions, he came across three Helmet Conchs in a triangular formation each about 16 feet (5 meters) away from the other two. Two were positioned properly to move around, but one was buried in the sand on its side, destined to death by predators or starvation as it would not be able to forage for food. Neville admits that it never occurred to him to turn this animal over because his mind was full of the recent observations from his swim, and he had to return to change film. He barely took notice of the three conchs except to observe their position. He assumed that other divers had gathered them on a boat and tossed them overboard after being informed that they were a protected species. A few hours later, with fresh air tanks and new film he made his way back and was amazed to see that the two conchs who were correctly positioned had moved closer to the one in trouble. Being a trained scientist, he sat back and observed the action. After approaching the one buried in the sand, "They had furrowed out a depression around the immobile shell, having dug away the sand as efficiently as if they were a pair of miniature bulldozers." He says: "I just didn't believe what might be happening, but I took the pictures anyway." As he watched in awe, after loosening the sand around the conch that was stuck, the two mobile conchs came around behind it, climbed up on the shell and toppled it over. Neville was nearly in tears as he witnessed, as he said, two "dumb, unfeeling invertebrates without vision or any known form of communication, with pea-sized 'brains' and no reasoning mechanism that we are aware of combine their actions to assist another of their species in trouble."

My first thought was how remarkably in sync this account was with the divination meaning of someone willing to fight for you. The behavior of the animal confirmed the meaning originally based upon the name and appearance of the shell. In quite dramatic contrast, after I read Neville's account of the Helmet Conchs, the headline story in my newspaper that night was about a woman in New York who was mugged. Despite her screams for help, everyone ignored her because they didn't want to get involved. I couldn't help but think that a Helmet Conch would devote hours to come to her rescue, *so which is the more evolved species*?

Let's consider this scene Neville witnessed. These conchs had to: (1) know a comrade was in trouble, (2) care enough to travel for hours to respond, (3) cooperate in figuring out a plan of action, then (4) carry it out—and, *they did*! Was this simply animal instinct? We can choose to believe that, or to believe that through compassion, intelligence, and dedication, that they accomplished a rescue that neither could have achieved alone.

Perhaps animals so obviously possess traits to which we aspire, that the only way we allow ourselves to be comfortable with their capacity for unconditional love is to label them as instinct. Otherwise, if animals possess this spiritual trait we desire, logic dictates that they are the more evolved beings, which many humans can't accept. But, what if a dog *does* have a choice whether to run into a burning building, or to dive into freezing waters to rescue a family member? These acts of love are then the genuine article, and dismissing them as instinct does us all a disservice. Wouldn't it be wonderful if the animals were mirroring our own potential, expressing the loving beings we really are?

When I first posed the question, "Who is the more evolved species?" comparing the conch to the people who ignored the mugging victim, I was leaning toward the conch. I have since come to believe that energetically we are all light beings. One of us comes to Earth and zips on a "human suit," another a "dog suit," another a "snail suit," but underneath we are all formed from the same source. At this energetic level, no being is above or below another on the evolutionary scale: we are all one. Instead of looking upon this demonstration of animal compassion as "less than" by evaluating and labeling a behaviors as "only instinct," why not see the gift they offer us, teaching us who we are—even in the behavior of a snail?

Despite Neville's knowledge that scientific methodology forbids interpreting animal behavior in terms of human emotions and values, I think he may have come to the same conclusions that I did. He ends his account with these words: "Regardless of how, or why, I saw two 'lowly invertebrates' spend several hours saving the life of another 'lowly invertebrate' and nobody on this planet is going to convince me otherwise."

With Neville Coleman's permission, I'm honored to share the photographs of this rescue (page 23) so that you can witness the act of these remarkable animals yourself and draw your own conclusions.

If the picture of the Helmet Conch on the front cover bothers you, this reflects concerns around trust. Since Helmet conchs demonstrate that they are willing to fight for you, if you dislike this shell, it means someone you thought would be willing to fight for you let you down, perhaps harming your capacity to trust. If a loved one can't be trusted, how can you trust anyone? When this occurs, you hesitate to delegate anything to others because that gives them the power to let you down. Instead, you take on every task yourself. In addition, if anyone asks you to do anything, you readily comply. After all, you know how it feels to be let down, and you would never want to create that pain in anyone else. Since there are only so many hours in the day, if you are unable to delegate, and unable to say no to requests from others, you are faced with a dilemma. The more work you take on, the greater the risk that your standards will start to suffer. Should this happen to you, please reevaluate your feelings about trust.

Horned Helmet Conchs
Cassis Cornuta

The conch in peril is on the left side of this photo. Two other conchs have approached the scene.

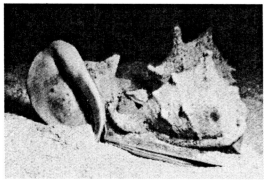

The two mobile conchs work like mini-bulldozers to loosen the sand around their stuck comrade.

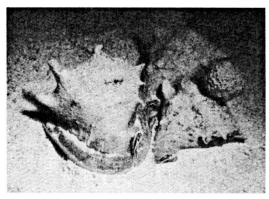

Once the endangered conch was no longer stuck, the other two made their way around its back, climbed up on the shell, and toppled it over.

Photographs taken by Neville Coleman copied with permission from his book *Shells Alive!* www.nevillecoleman.com.au

What's on Your Radar?

Throughout this book, I suggest that we uncover our hidden beliefs in order to grant us the opportunity to change anything that is no longer serving us. Time and again, I've watched my clients become aware of limiting beliefs, and then wonder how they go about transforming them? When they discover a limiting thought operating behind the scenes, they slowly encounter stimulating new ways of thinking to change it. For example, if you believe nobody is honest, than, as Sand Dollar teaches, it is possible that honest people have not been part of your experience thus far. Once you uncover the belief that no one is honest, if you desire to change it, you begin encountering examples that show this belief is false. Honest people may not be in your immediate environment, but you may slowly become aware honesty exists when you hear something on TV, or read a newspaper article, or even overhear someone's conversation describing a stranger making an honest choice. Now the possibility of someone being honest is on your radar. Once this occurs, you can start believing honest people exist. Then you can build on the foundation that they are "out there" and begin to draw honest people into your own life.

Let me demonstrate this principle using a reading involving the seahorse: For its role in the birth process, the male seahorse is remarkable in the animal kingdom. Though the female lays the eggs, the male is equipped with a pouch into which the eggs are transferred. There, they remain and are nurtured until his contractions release the infant seahorses into the ocean. This is as close as a male of any species comes to giving birth. Due to this behavior, seahorse represents the ideal nurturing male.

With *Ocean Oracle*, the image of the seahorse often brings warm smiles. Occasionally, the seahorse bothers someone. A client once pointed to the seahorse image exclaiming, "I hate seahorses." Her next comment left me stunned. "But they are like unicorns, they aren't real." Since seahorse represents the ideal nurturing male energy, the ideal husband or father, I wondered how she could ever have a healthy relationship with a male if she believed seahorses "aren't real." I was not surprised to discover that the men in her life, including her father and husband, were far from ideal. She was quite shocked when I informed her that seahorses do exist. When she inquired where they could be found, I told her that if she were not able to see them in their natural habitat in the ocean, not to despair. She could visit them in an aquarium. She then disclosed that she lived near an aquarium and visited it often…but she had never seen a seahorse. It occurred to me that if she thought they were mythological, she could be standing in front of their tank and not see them. This conversation was just what she needed to become aware of the fact that seahorses aren't imaginary. She planned to visit the aquarium the next day, and I knew she was about to see her first live seahorse. The beauty of this exchange is that by awakening to the idea that seahorses are real, she also opened to the concept of nurturing human males. This information enabled her to create from the new belief that men can be wonderful husbands and fathers. Such a simple recognition could completely transform her future.

Although I have yet to find other shell readers, I have encountered many shell speakers. Occasionally, someone is conscious of the fact that shells speak. More often, shell communication is subtle, occurring subconsciously. The shells are speaking volumes, but the person is unaware. The effect is like someone wearing earplugs while attending a symphony, or sitting in a classroom. He is positioned to receive beneficial information for his heart or mind, but oblivious to the fact that he is surrounded by it. If you have ever selected greeting cards with shells depicted on them, or are attracted to seashell décor, you may qualify as a member of this second category. When clients tell me about their favorite shell, or a shell they have at home, they are amazed to discover that its meaning relates to the very issue they find challenging.

To bear witness to this, let's travel back through time and visit the Wright Brothers' home. We are fortunate that in Michigan, at Henry Ford's Museum and village, Mr. Ford decided to preserve the homes and laboratories of the inventors of his day. With their permission, he literally uprooted these buildings and transplanted them in his village. Thomas Edison's home and laboratory are only yards away from the Wright Brothers' home and bike shop. As you enter each edifice, a staff member recites a brief history of its former occupants and answers questions. When I saw an arrangement of three large shells prominently displayed on the Wright Brothers' mantle, I asked "Are these their actual seashells?" I was informed that, indeed, these were their genuine shells. The Wright Brothers brought them back from Kitty Hawk.

On the mantle were a Helmet Conch, Nigrite Murex, and Pink Conch (front cover, numbers 34, 33, 32). Respectively, these shells mean "someone is willing to fight for you" (see page 21 for more on the Helmet Conch), "the courage to overcome negative emotions such as anger and depression," and "listen to your heart." At first look, these shells seem to be there to strengthen their fortitude and console the Wright Brothers in the face of tremendous opposition as they taught man to soar. The Helmet Conch would suggest that they had someone in their corner willing to encourage and support their efforts despite public ridicule.

Curious about the identity of who had been the "Helmet Conch" support in their life, I turned to the Internet and came across their relationship with Octave Chanute. Octave Chanute was a French-born American engineer who began studying aviation when he was in his fifties, and who was in his sixties when the energetic young Wright Brothers contacted him. Chanute thought that solving the multifaceted problems of aviation required the shared contributions of many researchers. He freely shared information with pioneers of flight, and when the Wright Brothers began their experimentation, they had all of Chanute's wisdom at their disposal. At a time when people interested in flight were considered crazy, he was their mentor, their friend, and supporter. He became their confidante as evidenced by "several hundred letters of correspondence touching on every phase and stage of aeronautical development." Here was their Helmet Conch! Now I wondered about the other shells. After their famous flight of 1903, the Wright brothers had changed the world. Was there deeper meaning to the Nigrite Murex and Pink Conch? As I read further, I learned that "patent disputes erupted in 1905 between (the Wright Brothers) and other flyers over aeronautical technology. Chanute broke off his correspondence with them at that time because he disagreed with their desire to control the technology of flight. For him, technical information was a public commodity, and he believed that the ability to fly would usher in a new age of enlightenment that the Wrights were thwarting." This could be the reason for the Nigrite Murex. The dissolution of their relationship with Chanute must have caused feelings of depression or anger. Whatever the emotional wounds, I wondered now about the Pink Conch: "Listen to your heart." As I continued reading, I discovered that the relationship was mending just before Chanute died in 1910. The brothers attended his funeral, and Wilbur Wright even delivered his eulogy. Perhaps those shells from Kitty Hawk, North Carolina, where Chanute had watched the Wright Brothers pursue their shared dream, were aiding them to heal in more ways than one.

My favorite of all the beliefs I present in this book is knowing the wonder and the magic of the Universe. The shells offer constant reminders of the magic at our disposal all the time. Magic, like the seahorse, is real. Keep it on your radar and it is only a matter of time before you experience it yourself. Let the miracles flow!

Shells as Energy Tools

Many people are familiar with crystal energy and its benefits for our mind, body and spirit. These crystals are from the *mineral* kingdom, and are connected to the *earth* element. As we evolve, our energy shifts, and new tools step forward to work with us. Seashells are ocean crystals created from the *animal* kingdom, and are connected to the *water* element. They have much to contribute alone or in combination with the crystals from the mineral kingdom. My seashell partners have kept their revelations synchronized with my own spiritual growth. I appreciate their patience waiting to unveil the healing power they hold in their matrix. This is energy available to all of you, and it is my pleasure to relate to you what they have shared with me.

Chakras

Any book dealing with the concept of energy dynamics should include a discussion of chakras. Our bodies are composed of many layers, the physical body being the densest of these. In addition, we possess subtle bodies composed of energy. Everything on the Earth plane is designed to teach you about your energy with the ultimate goal of bringing you to a state of love.

"Chakra" comes from the Sanskrit word for "wheel." Your energy, or light body, contains seven major chakras stacked from the base of the spine to just above your head. Each chakra is associated with a color, and an attribute. Chakras are a large, fascinating subject of study. For the purposes of this book, here's a brief outline to introduce or refresh the concept:

The first, or root, chakra is located at the base of your spine, and is associated with the color red. It connects to your right to be on the Earth, and survival issues.

The second chakra is associated with the color orange. It is located at hip level and is about your sexuality and creativity.

The third chakra is connected to the color yellow and is found in the solar plexus region. It connects to your personal will and self-image.

The fourth chakra is at the heart and is associated with the colors green or pink. It connects to love.

The fifth chakra is at the throat and is associated with the color blue. It is about expression, speaking your truth.

The sixth is at the level of your third eye, between your eyebrows. It is associated with the color violet, or indigo, and is about your connection to your intuition.

The seventh, or crown chakra, is just above your head. It is associated with the color white, gold, or silver and is where you connect to your Divinity.

As you will see, there are schools of thought that extend the chakras beyond these seven, but more about this later on.

Each chakra allows us great opportunities to explore who we are and to discover our truth. Along the way, it is possible for us to be wounded at any of these energy centers and experience blockages in our energy flow. For example, hesitancy to speak your truth can lead to problems in the throat chakra. If these are not addressed energetically, they become denser and eventually register in our physical body. Seashells have much to say about this subject. If you will turn the page, we can begin our instruction from these masterful teachers.

Chakra Shells
Abalone

Before I had knowledge of their connection to our chakras, the Abalone was about the need to heal emotionally or repressed emotional problems may affect you physically. This meaning derived from the combined physical contributions of the abalone mollusk as well as the emotional properties of the Abalone shell it creates and inhabits.

Look first at the Abalone shell, the play of light upon its crystalline structure creates an iridescent rainbow of hues. This panoramic display of colors attracts many admirers and the natural concave structure makes it a practical vessel for many purposes. Native Americans use the Abalone shell for smudging ceremonies in which sage is placed in the center of the Abalone bowl and set on fire. The smoke fumes produced cleanse the energy of any negativity. Thus, the Abalone shell assists in healing at an energetic, emotional level (inside back cover, photo 4A). The abalone mollusk contributes to healing. Extracts from this animal, called paolin, have been found to fight penicillin-resistant strains of staph, strep, and typhus. Through this medicine, the abalone mollusk connects healing to our physical body. Combined, the shell and mollusk offer healing from two sources: the emotional, energetic healing aided by the shell, and the physical healing from the animal's medicinal extracts.

Metaphysics teaches that our essence extends beyond the physical body in several energetic layers comprising our aura. Abalone instructs us that healing may be accomplished working from the outside emotional, energetic fields inward toward the physical body. If healing occurs at this level, we may circumvent physical illness. If healing is not accomplished at the outer level, the issue may manifest as a physical ailment. As much as people might wish it were otherwise, when emotions are repressed or denied, they do not disappear. They desire our attention, and if ignored at the emotional stage, they ask for our notice at the physical level. Working with Abalone is about learning to honor your emotions, not to repress them. They must surface to a level of awareness before they can heal.

As damaging as repressing emotional pain can be, so too can dwelling upon it. The central region of the shell containing the greatest concentration of swirling colors is the muscle scar where the animal was once attached—a vivid reminder of the wounds caused by attachment to unhealthy emotions. (See muscle scars on inside of shell, inside back cover, photo 4A.) If a person deals with surfaced emotions by attaching blame to others for her own misery ("it's your fault my life is a mess") she may deliberately sabotage her own success to show others how much they have damaged her life. If she succeeds, the people she blames are let off the hook. If she chooses to continue the cycle of blame, she ruins any chance of success for herself. Holding on to painful experiences, allowing them to fester, can wreak havoc upon the physical body.

You may have noticed that the Abalone shell has several holes along its edge. The animal forms these openings to excrete its waste products. This is the release point. The number of holes remains constant throughout its life and has no relationship to the size of the shell. Photo 3A on the inside back cover shows two three-hole Abalones maintaining the same number of holes although they are vastly different in size. As the animal grows and enlarges its shell, it seals off the innermost hole and builds a replacement at the outer edge. The holes serve as a reminder that we too must prepare continual outlets to release these emotionally charged issues. Although we can't heal the unhealthy waste in our lives without acknowledging it, we also do ourselves a disservice by hanging onto and revisiting it. Our friend, the Abalone, is here to work with us on many levels to acknowledge, heal, and release our pain as we grow into our truth.

Abalones as Chakra Tools

After calls from crystal workers asking how they might add shells to their work, I turned to meditation and asked the shells to guide me. I was shown an Abalone. Knowing next to nothing about energy centers at the time, I thought the Abalones could be employed at the top of the spine and at the bottom and that together they would somehow align the chakras. I was not clear at all on the details of how this would work, but I shared the feeling with a friend who was willing to experiment. The first attempts didn't work, and I wondered what I was missing from the vision in the meditation. During a sleepless night, I realized that one of my friend's shells had five holes, and one had three. As each Abalone adds a new hole while simultaneously plugging the oldest hole, it always maintains the original number of holes throughout its life. I had never paid attention to how many holes they had before. I immediately threw back my bed covers and rushed downstairs to see how many holes my Abalones had. To my amazement, I found shells in my collection containing three, four, six, and seven holes. I easily obtained one like my friend's with five. (See inside back cover, photos 3A, 4A, 5A, 6A, and 7A.) Such loyalty to a specific number of holes through deliberate genetic programming struck me as quite significant. I was seeking a method for energy workers to use shells, and my one bit of knowledge at the time was that there were seven chakras. I postulated that the number of holes in an Abalone corresponds to a specific chakra, or energy center, in our body. If Abalones were about the need to heal emotionally, perhaps a particular Abalone was connected to healing at the level of a particular chakra. I considered the possibility that they would assist healing at the solar plexus (three), heart (four), throat (five), third eye (six), and crown (seven). Working with shells is a constant work in progress!

Quick to admit that this was new territory for me, I used my seashell divination column in *The Kaleidoscope Journal*, a metaphysical magazine, to ask for readers to experiment with Abalones by matching the number of holes to a particular chakra, and to report any feedback—good, bad, or indifferent. (I cautioned that if an Abalone had a partial hole at the outer edge, not to count it because by the time it is complete, the animal would have plugged its innermost hole.)

The results were dramatic. Readers wrote in and shared experiences that served to strengthen my belief in this discovery; some of which are related below. Additional validation came from aura photography. A willing photographer allowed her young son to hold various Abalones while he was connected to the aura equipment. He was unaware of the point of this experiment, but content to play. At the time, I had three-, four-, five-, six-, and seven-hole Abalones. First, he was randomly handed a four-hole Abalone, which according to the theory, should relate to the heart chakra. We watched in awe when his image on the monitor alternated colors. A large patch of green appeared. A bit astonished, the photographer whispered to me that green is the color registered by the heart chakra. Likewise, holding the three-hole Abalone produced yellow shadings and the five-hole produced bluer shadings. These were all in keeping with the corresponding chakra colors on the aura photography machine.

One-Hole Abalone (inside back cover, photo 1A)

When I began my shell divination column in *The Kaleidsocope*, I believed that everything I said regarding shells required proof. I stayed as firmly rooted in science as possible. Slowly, hints of intuition crept into my work. I reached a crossroads when I proposed the experiment with Abalones to explore the possibility that they connected to specific chakras. Alternating between the role of teacher and student, encouraging feedback that resonated at every level allowed me to open myself to what the shells could teach beyond science. Letting go of the science was not an easy choice, but it allowed my personal spiritual growth to reach new heights.

I realized for the chakra theory to be true, there had to be a one-hole Abalone, This seemed unlikely because if the holes are where the animal excretes its waste, what self-respecting abalone would only give itself one hole? While pondering this, I was blessed by the opportunity to become a presenter on the *Sea Angels Psychic Cruise*. This included the privilege of teaching seashell divination on the Cayman Islands. Not wanting to risk damaging my shells, I contented myself with photographs for most of them, but, eager to share this new energy connection with the cruise guests, I also took my Abalone collection.

To my amazement, on the cruise—on the very day of my seminar—my husband and I casually stepped in to a jewelry store to cool down, and I came across a one-hole Abalone! I would have paid dearly for that precious shell, but it only cost $5.00. A few minutes later, I headed off to teach my workshop with complete faith in the information I was about to impart. At the proper moment I shared my newest prize, delighting the cruise guests when I turned over the one-hole Abalone revealing brilliant swatches of red.

Two-Hole Abalone (inside back cover, photo 2A)

A friend mailed me a two-hole Abalone she found displayed by a shell merchant in a Michigan mall. This particular species was from Viet Nam. Upon turning it over, I was astounded to discover the predominate streaks of orange covering the exterior surface. How appropriate since orange is the color connected to the second chakra.

Three-Hole Abalone (inside back cover, photo 3A)

When I appealed to *The Kaleidoscope* readers, several with three-hole Abalones wrote about experiencing third chakra challenges with self worth. We can learn much from one story in particular, in which Steve was eager to go camping, but was low on funds. He needed many supplies because he was looking for lightweight gear to ease his burden during the long hike. He researched carefully to find the articles that would suit his needs, then went shopping. While in a store looking at winter clothing for the trip, he ventured downstairs to look at their sleeping bags. He saw the very sleeping bag he wanted and asked the sales person what he could tell him about it. The sales person told him it was the last one in stock, and was on sale for $39. Surprised that this item which normally cost four times that amount could be $39, he asked "Are you sure?" The salesman showed him the sale card, which was marked $39.00. When Steve arrived at the cash register, the sleeping bag rang up at $160.00. He handed the sales card to the cashier, who called the salesman. As this occurred, a line was forming at the register, and Steve became concerned that he would look dishonest in front of all of these people. When the salesman arrived, questioned by the cashier, he back peddled and called the manager, who said the price was a mistake. Instead, he offered a twenty percent discount off the sleeping bag price. After purchasing the sleeping bag, Steve asked God what that had been about? He was shown a vision of the manager sitting with a pile of money, and he was asked "Do you think that slight amount of money you would save would change that man's world at all? God brings gifts in strange ways—do not discount the gift." Steve realized that his personality so feared the judgment of the people in line that he began questioning his right to deserve the sleeping bag at such a low cost, and he lost the energy of the gift. He spent many months working on healing the battle between "my will" versus. "Thy will."

The following year, he had researched flat screen TVs. Again, because of financial constraints, he traveled to another state to avoid paying the additional sales tax. In the store, he found the TV he wanted, but the salesman who approached him said, "Are you buying this just to make you feel good to have it hang on your wall? You don't want this." This time, Steve did not argue. He took it as a sign to trust and surrender, and he left the store. That evening, he received an e-mail from a friend informing him of a code that he could use to save twenty percent on the TV. The next day, he returned to the store and thanked the salesman who made him delay his purchase so he could save over $300. The difference between the way he felt about the TV and the way he felt about the sleeping bag allowed a different outcome. Steve surrendered his pride about his self-image and discovered that the TV could come to him in an even better way than he had expected. This small lesson reinforced his conviction that surrendering brings more than his personality could ever imagine. He now lives his life reaping the rewards of letting go. No longer limited by financial worries, he simply does as he is guided. When needs arise, his spiritual work dovetails perfectly to provide the funds. As he told me, "If you live your life making it what you think it should be, there is no room for God."

Four-Hole Abalone (inside back cover, photo 4A)

Four-hole Abalones relate to healing problems rooted in feeling unlovable. Since the four-hole was my first Abalone, it came as no surprise when I learned it was the Abalone most people reported having. One woman shared that she had recently moved to a new home, and was frustrated because she couldn't find her Abalone shell after she unpacked. She thought she left it in her basement where she planned to use it to smudge the area to cleanse the energy. Once I told her about the other uses of Abalone, I suggested that it may want to be in her life for a purpose other than smudging. I received a telephone call a few days later. She was laughing because she found her Abalone. It was a four-hole Abalone, and she found it waiting for her in her bedroom.

Five-Hole Abalone (inside back cover, photo 5A)

Feedback involving five-hole Abalones reveals struggles with major throat ailments. One dramatic encounter occurred during a workshop in Florida when a woman named Julie handed me her favorite Abalone shell with pieces of other shells inside it. The Abalone had five holes, and she asked me why I thought she only collected pieces of the other shells to store in it. I observed that the other shells related to inspiration and happiness, but because she only had a fragment of each shell, it was as if she would not allow herself the full measure of the joy and inspiration in her life. Since five-hole Abalones correspond to the throat chakra, this would hold especially true as it relates to her voice. It was possible that she had difficulty speaking her truth, which kept her from complete happiness. I asked if she ever had throat problems. She revealed that she was in a serious accident when she was fifteen years old, resulting in a month-long coma. Her long road to recovery left her with partially paralyzed vocal cords, creating a voice that was barely a whisper. Through hard work, she has regained her speaking voice, but can no longer raise her voice or yell. I asked if she ever wished she could yell? She admitted that it would be useful in an emergency. That seemed limited to me, so I asked if she ever got angry? She first replied "No," then she admitted that there were times she wanted to yell but she felt she needed to hold everything inside. She described herself as meek. We discovered that she believed that in order to be loved, she had to hold her tongue. It was amazing to see that the accident insured that she would never raise her voice. We discussed the fact that even if an emotion is repressed, it does not disappear. Abalone teaches that it still impacts your life.

Four years later, when writing this section of the book, I found Julie's contact information, and called to see what this revelation brought to her life. Due to her surgery, she is still not able to raise her voice, but she shared a remarkable alternative she had found: Following a very frustrating time in her life, she created a mandala (symbolic art design) that she said resembled an open mouth that looked like it was screaming. She connected this to her father who had committed suicide. She had never fully grieved the death of her father, and had held in a great deal of anger. I reminded her that anger is one of the stages of grief, and suggested that she needed to express her anger to be able to move on to achieve acceptance. This conversation allowed her to see that the screaming mandala was a way for her to express her own pent up anger. She has continued to joyfully express herself through her mandala artwork. She informed me that she feels insecure when she begins drawing her mandalas, but by the time she adds color, they flow out of her. The tentative drawing is like her whispers, but the flowing color is her way to holler with rage or glee. She understood that although she cannot fully express herself with her voice, her mandalas have offered her a wonderful substitute.

During this update, she also commented on her tendency to only find pieces of shells. Even when she found them whole, by the time she got them home, they would have broken into pieces. Then one day, after a long car trip, she was amazed to discover a fully intact Starfish in her car. For her, this was quite significant. Not only did she have no idea how it got into her car, but it was whole! I found her next comment to be very telling: She wished she could put down roots somewhere, because she "felt so fragmented." No wonder she only found pieces of shells; she herself was in pieces. She also spoke of feeling victimized, keeping silent all her life, and wished she could go through a rebirth. Then she recognized the uplifting message from that intact Starfish inside her car. It indicated that an enormous shift had taken place: she had increased the full measure of her survival, no longer functioning from the role of silent victim, and she just needed to be made aware of it.

Six-Hole Abalone (inside back cover, photo 6A)

Those who have shared their six-hole Abalone stories with me have been struggling with third eye issues, meaning situations that challenged them to trust their inner senses over their physical eyes and ears. We read earlier how the shaman was able to see Columbus' ships with his inner vision. One client who was working with the six-hole Abalone disclosed that as she was developing deeper intuitive abilities, she noticed her physical vision was suffering. Working with the Abalone, she realized that she thought in order to deserve to be a good "seer," it required a trade off with her physical vision. Uncovering this hidden belief allowed her to reframe her feelings about the need for this sacrifice. In a very short time, she realized how this belief caused her to benefit from poor vision as the price she paid for stronger inner vision. Recognizing this, she was able to reevaluate her position, and allow herself to have great psychic abilities without having to be at the expense of her physical vision. Since this revelation, she happily reported that her eyeglass prescription has been steadily decreasing.

Seven-Hole Abalone (inside back cover, photo 7A)

Working from the seventh chakra, we perceive that there is something grander than our human selves; we learn of the possibility of our Divinity. The inspirational poem "Footprints in the Sand," by Mary Stevenson, is an excellent example of how this anger at God can impact our lives without our awareness. Dreams can reveal our subconscious feelings and this poem relates the following dream:

> *One night I dreamed I was walking along the beach with the Lord.*
> *Many scenes from my life flashed across the sky.*
> *In each scene I noticed footprints in the sand.*
> *Sometimes there were two sets of footprints,*
> *other times there were one set of footprints.*
>
> *This bothered me because I noticed*
> *that during the low periods of my life,*
> *when I was suffering from*
> *anguish, sorrow or defeat,*
> *I could see only one set of footprints.*
>
> *So I said to the Lord,*
> *"You promised me Lord,*
> *that if I followed you,*
> *you would walk with me always.*
> *But I have noticed that during the most trying periods of my life*
> *there have only been one set of footprints in the sand.*
> *Why, when I needed you most, have you not been there for me?"*

This is how the person who feels separate can perceive being abandoned by God. But, the poem continues:

> *The Lord replied,*
> *"The times when you have seen only one set of footprints in the sand,*
> *is when I carried you."*

This is the message of the seven-hole Abalone. To bring the healing that although you feel abandoned, or betrayed by God, your connection was never severed.

I also have a personal experience to share on this topic. At the request of Casslyn, the crystal worker, I once made a shell grid to help her with some energy work. It covered the entire top of my dining room table, and among the shells in my grid was the tusk shell that means "someone who appears to be heartless." The next day I discovered the tusk shell had fallen on the floor and was broken in half. I thought it odd that no other shell fell, but assumed my cat must have played with it and knocked it off. I put the pieces away intending to repair it, but I couldn't find any suitable glue. When I asked my husband if we had any more, he said that he would pick some up for me later when he went out to do errands. Later that day, I visited a Tarot website and decided to have a reading. As I turned over the cards, they spoke of great anger at God, which moved me to tears because I realized I had, indeed, been very angry at God for quite some time. I sat with my Abalone and came to understand that God was not the source of my problem. I had created the situation I was in. As a final healing, I went to sit with the grid I had made for Casslyn. Then I remembered the tusk shell: "Someone who was heartless." I never expected that to be God. I decided to repair the shell and place it back in the grid. When I went to retrieve the two pieces, they were no longer broken. The shell was intact. Thinking my husband must have repaired it, I went downstairs to thank him. His response shocked me. He had not left yet to buy the glue, and he did not even know where I had stored the broken pieces of the shell. To this day, I don't know how the shell was repaired. What I do know is that it broke to get my attention that I was angry at God being heartless, and once I healed that belief, the shell was no longer broken.

Nine-Hole Abalone (Inside back cover, photos 9A and 9B)

To best illustrate the significance of the Abalones, we should first jump from seven to nine holes. When I first received a nine-hole Abalone, as aesthetically beautiful as it was, my heart sank. As far as I knew, there were only seven chakras and I thought that this find disproved the connection between chakras and Abalones. Before I announced that, however, I summoned all the courage I had, and took the nine-hole Abalone to a shaman friend, knowing that he would speak the truth. I steeled myself for disappointing news, but instead received an education in chakras. Apparently, there are many more than the seven main chakras.

When he took the Abalone from me, my friend immediately felt drawn to hold it above his head. He likened it to a doorway to other realms. Another energy worker told me she felt it connected people to past lives, and could be an effective scrying tool. (Scrying is a practice of using an object such as a crystal as a medium for aiding in divination.) Yet another felt connected to angelic beings. Everyone who sees this Abalone comments on the muscle scar. You can see the top portion of a skull and some see a couple of white buffalo defined in the iridescent interior. The Abalone-chakra theory remains intact.

A Unique Four-Hole Abalone (Inside back cover, photo 4B)

Meeting the unique four-hole Abalone turned my world upside down. Sitting on a friend's vendor's table at a psychic fair was an unassuming Abalone. When I picked it up for a closer inspection, I was astonished to find it had four holes, but the holes stopped with a good two inches of solid shell growth beyond them. Since Abalones use these holes to eliminate waste, they continue forming holes throughout their shell's growth—just as when we grow there is always something new to process and release. In fact, I thought that when we finally did heal everything, we left the planet.

I admit this Abalone had me perplexed. It defied all logic. I stared at it, transfixed. It was declaring that after healing at the level of the heart chakra it had nothing more to release. There was no more waste to process. And, miracle of miracles, after it healed everything it continued to live. Prior to meeting this Abalone, I had never entertained the possibility that we can heal everything and continue to function on this planet. How wonderful to be able to go about our service unencumbered by any more of our own "stuff." I want to share this with you in the desire that it will fill you with the same hope it gave me.

Ten-Hole Abalone (Inside back cover, photo 10A)

I was offered a marvelous opportunity to teach on St. Croix, Virgin Islands. The invitation came through Casslyn Allen, president of *Symphonies of the Heart*, an energetics consulting firm. Casslyn is the crystal worker mentioned in the introduction who had originally contacted me to teach her how to add shells to her energy work. Although I was completely ignorant about this process, her faith in my ability to discover the information she sought was tantalizing. I shared each bit of progress as it revealed itself to me. Now, almost two years later, I would be granted the privilege of teaching an all-day workshop in the Caribbean. Talk about heaven! I immediately began dreaming of what I could do with an entire day to teach. In deep gratitude to Casslyn, I sent away for a special gift. Having witnessed her wonder at my nine-hole Abalone, I wanted to present her with one of her own. What arrived was not what I asked for at all. In its place was the most incredible Abalone I have ever seen. It had ten holes, but most remarkable to me was the fact that it lacked any muscle scar. As a brief review, the scar forms where the animal's muscle attaches its body to its shell. I wondered how it could be possible for an Abalone shell to contain no scar.

In shell divination, Abalones are about acknowledging emotions so they do not have to gain attention at the physical level. The scar formed from attachment cautions that once feelings are confronted, it is not healthy to attach to these emotions. Some people sabotage their own success by blaming others or circumstances for ruining their lives. The Abalone encourages us to forgive, with the goal to heal and release these emotions. The fact that this ten-hole Abalone possessed no scar reveals an incarnated being who understood that there is nothing to forgive. If the number of holes equates to the chakras, this ten-hole Abalone has progressed beyond individual consciousness and is connected to the Oneness. It is capable of seeing the big picture, and at that level, it comprehends that everything happens as it should. I began to recognize that the true lesson of forgiveness is not about achieving the ability to forgive, but understanding that there is nothing to forgive.

In the weeks prior to my departure for St. Croix, I showed this shell to everyone who touched my life. Without fail, each person interacting with it had a profound experience. Now I was faced with a moral dilemma. As grateful as I was for the opportunity to teach on the Island, I did not want to give this shell away. In an effort to obtain another, I wrote to the proprietor of the store who shipped it to me. I asked him what species this was, and did every Abalone of this species lack muscle scars? I was surprised to hear that when I asked for a nine-hole Abalone he had nothing in his store inventory, but that something had drawn him to search through an unsorted box of shells he had found in storage, and that this shell had been in there. It came with no description, and he hadn't noticed the absence of a muscle scar.

I could only marvel at these extraordinary circumstances: the ten-hole Abalone shell remained packed away in storage until it found its way to me when I placed an order requesting a gift for someone else. It occurred to me that if it had arrived any sooner, I would not have reached a level of spiritual growth to understand and appreciate its message. I took it to St. Croix, and it was greeted with the same awed response as it received with everyone back home. I confessed to Casslyn that it came to me due to my seeking a gift for her, but I was having difficulty parting with it. She sympathized, and had the great insight that it was a tool for her work on the Island while I was there, but then it needed to return with me to be available for others. While in St. Croix, I attended a workshop on *A Course in Miracles*. What perfect timing that the lesson that night was "God does not forgive because God does not condemn." It was the message from the ten-hole Abalone speaking loud and clear.

A few weeks later, I was working at a Whole Health Expo, and had it displayed on my table. About midway through the day, I found myself categorically listing all my faults to an unsuspecting visitor at my booth. Surprised by this litany I was releasing, I looked down and had to smile. There was the ten-hole Abalone directly in front of me. Because it provides the energy of understanding there is nothing to blame and nothing to forgive, I felt safe to acknowledge my flaws and release any attachment they held for me. I will grant you that the timing could have been better, and I immediately explained to the confused visitor how the Abalone worked. She wisely took it to a private place to experience its interaction herself.

Eight-Hole Abalone (Inside back cover, photos 8A and 8B)
By the time I possessed Abalones with one, two, three, four, five, six, seven, nine, and ten holes, it stood to reason that an eight-hole Abalone must exist. Considering the miraculous ways some of the others

made their way to me, I was confident an eight-hole Abalone would come into my life to complete my collection. Word went out to everyone I knew to keep their eyes peeled during their travels. Eventually, I received two eight-hole Abalones courtesy of separate individuals.

I had learned that the first seven chakras connect to our physical body, the ninth chakra revolves around past lives and other dimensions, and the tenth chakra is about being connected to Oneness. I recognized that the eighth must be the bridge we cross when looking beyond our human conditioning to incorporate higher dimensions of self.

While working with the nine-hole Abalone, when my perspective on life shifted dramatically; I started to expand beyond my identity as "human" and began thinking in less limited terms. While swimming in the Caribbean one day, I suddenly knew that I could walk on water. Although I had no doubt that the feeling had been true, my frustration increased when later I couldn't remember how to accomplish it. The next day, while swimming with friends, I swam toward a looming coral wall, thinking it presented no obstacle because I could just disassemble and reassemble on the other side. My friends' warning screams snapped me out of my reverie before I crashed into the wall. I was mystified. What had possessed me to think I could function as anything other than a solid physical human being? These were certainly not typical thoughts and I wondered if there was "something in the water."

Without my realizing it, the disconnection from my limited human perspective had intensified with the energy of my ten-hole Abalone. I saw us as light beings who zip on a costume to "play" at being a human, or bird, or dog, but underneath we were all equal. As the connection to our spiritual body and the Oneness strengthens through the ninth and tenth chakras, it can become enticing to separate from our human identities. I think many of us are taught that the more we open our upper chakras, the more spiritually evolved we become. The Bible describes this as "being in the world but not of it," a perspective that implies that continuing to function from the lower chakras would somehow taint our spiritual evolution.

Enter the eight-hole Abalone, quietly reflecting my belief that opening the eighth chakra provides a bridge to energies outside all familiar human conditioning. This belief made me subconsciously try to disconnect from my human vessel. In eighth-chakra terms, I was crossing the bridge away from my human self toward the ninth and tenth chakras. My physical body tried to warn me by pleading for attention as best it could. In a matter of months, I had eye surgery, back problems, and a car accident. Still, I was so resolute in my journey toward the upper chakras, I thought these experiences were designed to put me out of commission so I could form a deeper connection with my spirit.

Just as I recovered from the car accident, a neighbor rang my doorbell. When I opened the door, he thrust out his hand and asked "Is this what you need?" He was holding a second eight-hole Abalone. I wondered why I needed another eight-hole Abalone if I had already crossed the bridge to these higher realms. I looked upon my neighbor's gift as an indication that I had missed something vital about the energies of the eighth chakra.

Chakra energies do not remain localized. They are in constant communication with each other, so every chakra contains a bit of the energies of every other chakra. As with people, what enhances one enhances all. As one chakra expands, it feeds the rest. When one is blocked, it limits the rest from functioning to their fullest capacity. Depending upon our beliefs, the energy generated at any particular chakra ebbs and flows. Likewise, the Abalone energies interact with each other. I must admit that I had great difficulty incorporating the ten-hole Abalone into my life. Its principle is Oneness, a state in which there is nothing to forgive. At first I wasn't able to communicate this information in a way that was useful to my clients. Instead of finding comfort in the idea that there is nothing to forgive it was hurtful to people who had been traumatized by others and fought to reach a place of forgiveness; despite my good intentions, the suggestion was perceived as a devaluing of their journeys.

The challenge of integrating this information eased when I worked with the new eight-hole Abalone—I had only understood part of the eighth chakra's lesson. The new shell helped me realize that the eighth chakra is a bridge, but its purpose is not to journey to the land of the upper chakras leaving behind our human identity, but to bring them back to join hands with the first seven. As I spoke to clients about the lessons from the nine- and ten-hole Abalones, the words were not resonating for them because I was too disconnected from the seven chakras of the physical body. To be coming from my heart, I needed my fourth chakra and to be speaking a truth that they could hear I needed my fifth chakra.

With this revelation, I reconnected with the chakras of my physical body and was then able to reengage with my light body. The eighth chakra energies allow us to integrate all parts of ourselves so that our spiritual, emotional, mental, and physical selves can function in this human body. All are of equal value.

The energies of the ninth and tenth chakras connect us to advanced spiritual concepts and wisdom permitting us to discard old notions of our identity and replace them with greater awareness and psychic abilities. As we open our eighth chakra we engage in the work required to unite these parts into a transformed whole being complete in a way we had never imagined. Instead of being in the world *but* not of it, we learn to be in the world *and* not of it. Processing and integrating the lessons learned from the ninth and tenth chakras, purifies us so we can release old patterns that kept us functioning from our physical, fear-based conditioning, and accelerate our spiritual growth.

Based on everything I now know, I feel confident the connection between chakras and Abalone has been clearly demonstrated. In my quest for answers, the Abalones have taken me beyond my wildest imaginings to a world of joyous possibilities. It gives me tremendous pleasure to be able to share this final outcome with you.

Interactions

We can now revisit earlier shell lessons to see how the chakra energies intertwine to enhance the shells' messages. Integration of the upper chakras introduces an entirely new way to interpret what keeps us secure when applied to the first lesson of Starfish and Survival. (See page 2.) From this perspective, because our physical identity gains equal value with our light bodies, security no longer exclusively pertains to physical health, financial stability, and a roof over our head. Although these remain vital, other factors contribute equally to our security. When considering survival, knowing that we are part of the Oneness, and that we exist in other dimensions of self can soothe what is commonly the greatest fear: death. With increased comprehension, we can appreciate that we are energy and that energy can't be destroyed—therefore we do not cease to exist. On a daily basis, recognizing that we are surrounded by Universal love provides access to inner peace.

Our material security manifests from our connection to our Divinity. How many of us have had this experience? We leave our homes to go about our daily business, and somewhere along the way encounter someone with a horrible cold. Our defenses go up, because we are programmed to believe that exposure to someone with a cold threatens our well-being. I experienced this all my life until I met someone who had multiple personalities. The personality who greeted me had a full-blown cold and could barely speak through her misery of runny nose, watery eyes, and cough. I was silently upset she had not warned me, and was sure I was doomed to catch her cold. I barely had time for this thought to register when she alternated her personality. To my amazement, every symptom vanished. This was the same human body, but the cold only affected one personality. Clearly this was evidence that the cold was not in the body, but in the mind. With this knowledge, I decided not to allow my human conditioning to follow its usual routine of creating a cold just because I was in the company of someone else who had one. My test came when my husband arrived home with a terrible cold. He suffered for days, but for the first time ever, even sleeping in the same bed did not result in my joining him in this agony. Understanding how we create, connecting with my Divinity, aided me in reprogramming my thoughts to choose a different experience for my body.

With our knowledge of this eighth chakra, take the lesson of Victimization and the Sand Dollar (see page 3) one more step. Although we create our reality, this does not occur in a vacuum. We are all in this together. What enhances one enhances all, and what belittles one belittles all. It is beneficial to realize that polarization of any kind is of our own making. Functioning from an "us vs. them" mentality interferes with us creating the paradise we seek. If people believe that in order for a privileged position to exist an underprivileged position must exist, too, this thought process creates separation and neither the "haves" (privileged) nor the "have-nots" (underprivileged) benefit. The "have-nots" perceive lack and powerlessness and so are unable to create their paradise. However, though they might have more, the privileged who devote their energy to defending and guarding their position, are not truly free to create either. Anyone who requires the perception of superiority creates from fear.

As the *Course in Miracles* states, "Nothing real can be threatened." If the privilege requires vigilance to safeguard, it is only illusion anyway. The truth is that there is more than enough for everyone. However, to manifest a world beyond polarity requires changing our beliefs regarding our identity as human beings. This is where crossing the bridge at the eighth chakra can lead: to the level playing field where all are welcome to contribute manifestations from their Divine selves. Then, as the lesson of the Wide-Mouthed Purpura shell (Feeling Special) suggests, we will live an ordinary life in a superior realm as our natural birthright. In a realm where everyone is aware that each new development enhances the whole, we would cherish the maximum growth potential of each member of our planet. Liberated to explore our truths, all of us would flourish. But fortunately, each of us can flourish individually, whether or not anyone else knows this or not. When I began to sense the power beliefs exert over experience, my friends would tell me that I just had to accept the way things were. But I could not see how the world could ever change if I contributed energy to the status quo. At that time I thought I had to hold the vision until others joined in and helped me create this realm. Now, I believe the realm always exists and we join it in our own time. It is for each of us to discover ourselves.

In a similar vein, all the other lessons take on new qualities when viewed from the eighth chakra. Feeling Flawed related to feeling limited in our knowledge of who we are. The ultimate Hero's Journey is crossing this bridge to integrate all parts of ourselves. The lesson of Surrender allows us to transcend beyond our human conditioning. If we are only functioning from the first seven chakras, we only serve from our humanness. If we align with "Thy will" when engaging all chakras, then if God wants us to serve by walking on water or uniting with a thorn bush in Oneness, we will. All of the love lessons shift when we see ourselves as light beings and we understand that love is the essence of who we are. Most of us have been searching for love; opening our eighth chakra will connect us to a love beyond human bounds. Our perceptions of beauty and our judgments also transform with a spiritual appreciation for everything on the planet. Seeing the magic in mucus, or reserving judgment concerning the poisons in our environment, comes from an understanding surpassing our human perspective.

If you are reading this, some part of your being is ready to gain awareness of your full potential. Don't look now, but conceding the possibility that the Helmet Conchs are intelligent and compassionate beings already alters your human conditioning. If the Perceptions of Beauty lesson inspired you to look at the world from alternative perspectives, you have painlessly transformed even more. If you choose it, the bridge to integration is a mere step away.

Lessons of Oneness, Tsunami Thoughts

In December of 2004, powerful earthquakes off the coast of Indonesia catapulted the ocean to launch gigantic waves of destruction that took 200,000 lives. Scientists call this event a tsunami. A grieving world was desperate for explanations. Since the ocean was the agent of this massive devastation, it was natural to think the shell kingdom might have some insights.

As I had been writing a shell divination column for *The Kaleidoscope Journal* for four years, some people had cast me in the role of ambassador to the seashell kingdom. Although uncomfortable with this mantle, I was not surprised when the editor of *The Kaleidoscope* called. If the shells ever needed someone to be their voice, this would be the time. I explained to my editor that I would love to, but I could not write on demand—it had to come from my heart. He understood, and with that burden lifted, I traveled as far out of my comfort zone as possible to try to hear what the shells had to say. Through the silence I heard one word: *Opportunity.* Then I heard *Remember your lessons.* At the time, I was immersed in the lessons of the ten-hole and eight-hole Abalones featuring energy concepts of oneness and integration. After a brief pause, a soft whisper instructed *You are looking through human eyes. Look through the ocean's eyes.*

We have seen man use the Earth as his play-toy without paying attention to the consequences. But gazing through the eyes of the ocean, I observed a new concern. I witnessed a vision repeated countless times throughout history: people lining up to be baptized in the ocean expecting the waters to wash our sins away. Recently I learned that in other cultures the ocean Goddess Yemaya cleanses our negativity by washing it away. I thought about that. Throughout time, we have journeyed to rivers, streams, or oceans asking to be cleansed. Since all water eventually flows to the ocean, she has become a repository for all our dark energies. Even if we are land-locked, it is the same energetic cycle. Our cries to be washed clean remove the impurities from our energy field, but deposit them energetically in the ocean's field. Her arms caress us, remove our sources of pain and misery, and carry them to her depths. But the ocean has been polluted with these energies without any way to become cleansed herself. Where is the balance? We expect her to store our negativity, but we never return to send her positive energy to replenish herself. When do we visit the ocean to offer our love or joy to her?

You may be aware of Masuro Emoto and his water crystal studies showing how our thoughts affect water. In his book, *The Hidden Messages in Water*, he documented scientific experiments exposing water to thoughts of love or hatred. The crystal formations took on the appearance of beautiful snowflake-like structures when exposed to thoughts of love, but the water could only muster amorphous blobs when exposed to hate. I attended a seminar he gave on this subject where he demonstrated water's reaction to photographs. If shown a pagoda, the crystals would mimic the same curvature of the structure; if shown an elephant picture, the crystals would form tusk-like shapes. I was awed as I realized that the water mimicked what it saw; it clearly has intelligence. It is a being that we have neglected for far too long.

The voice had also said to remember my lessons. I had no answers, only thoughts to contemplate. The ocean is a light being, as are we. The lesson of oneness teaches that there is no separation. We are the ocean, and the ocean mirrors what we have become. It reflects the negative energy accumulated in our own bodies from the anger and hatred in the world. Together, we all created this oceanic being capable of destroying more than 200,000 lives. We must be careful to not send all our grief and fear to the ocean, but to send it love in order to heal. Just as we need to send love to each other.

To be proactive, it might be nice to reverse roles. Let's go to the ocean to remove some of her pain. We put it there, she has stored it faithfully, and now we can transform it through our love. At the very least, let's become conscious of the need for balance. While she continues to accept our negativity, we can intercede before this reaches critical mass. We can form a partnership where the ocean cleanses us when we are weak, and where we send her love and gratitude when we are strong. In his seminar, Dr. Emoto suggested to tell the water in our life "I love you and appreciate you, Water." We can do this whenever we take a shower. Since our bodies are mostly water, these thoughts become who we are. Increasing our capacity to love, thinking loving thoughts, might change what we see reflected in the ocean's mirror and rescue all of us in the process.

Beyond the Tenth Chakra

Up until this point, I have held that an Abalone maintains the number of holes it has throughout its life. As discussed in the previous pages, its DNA seems to code for this. True to form, just as I became comfortable with this theory, an Abalone arrived to push me out of my comfort zone. After witnessing the four-hole Abalone that ceased making holes, and the ten-hole Abalone with no muscle scar, I have learned nothing an Abalone does is impossible. However, this new Abalone pushed my understanding of energy to an unprecedented level, and with its teachings, I have entered an entirely new realm of possibilities. This Abalone transformed from an eleven-hole to a twelve-hole seemingly overnight, and some people have seen the makings of a thirteenth hole. I readily admit that I have no explanation for how this Abalone shell was able to change its structure when it was devoid of any physical animal—the being supposedly responsible for making the holes. All I can do is report what I have observed.

Since writing my first book, I have been blessed with many generous readers who have taken the time to contact me expressing their appreciation for the information. With one such reader in Hawaii, our conversation led to the new information about Abalones. A few days later, she sent me an e-mail describing her chance arrival at, of all places, a seashell store, when she had pulled over simply to avoid traffic. There, she found a nine-hole Abalone, a ten-hole, and an eleven-hole. My Abalone collection did not exceed ten holes, so I asked her to please let me know what she learned working with the eleven-hole Abalone. When she wrote me that she had bought one for me, I felt it represented a new spiritual initiation, and imagined what it would bring to my life. When it arrived, I got quite the surprise: it was not an eleven-hole Abalone, it had twelve holes. The twelfth hole was on the outer lip of the Abalone where a new hole should form, but the curious thing is that it had taken a different direction from the other eleven. The others are all in a row on one plane, but then the pattern suddenly bends, placing this twelfth hole on a different plane. (See the inside back cover, photos 12A and 12B.)

The first night I worked with it, I had a dream. I was told to place an object in my right hand, and one in my left hand, and to close my eyes. My right hand grasped a juicy red apple, and my left encircled a gleaming Cowrie shell. Then I was told to open my eyes and allow myself to be surprised by what was in my right hand and then told to be surprised by what was in my left hand. I found these requests ridiculous since I knew what I had placed in each hand. How could I be surprised? And then I understood. By assuming I already knew what was there, I left no room for it to change. Holding the energy of possibility allows people and events to grow and teach us something new. The Abalone was a living example of this. It was supposed to be 11 holes, and when I checked with the person who sent it, she shared an even greater surprise. Here is what she told me in her own words.

When I first found the elevens I found two of them. I brought home a nine, ten, and an eleven for me, and a ten and eleven for another friend. When I got them out I thought, "Oh, I must have miscounted." There were one eleven, two tens and two nines. I went back to the shell shop to look for two more elevens, but only found one. Then I got ready to mail the shells out (I was planning to keep searching for an eleven for my other friend, or give her mine). I had been careful counting them; holding them up to the light to be sure it was a hole I was looking at and not just a spot. And I kept them organized in groups. I must have counted them over a dozen times to be sure I had it right. The morning I packed them for mailing—I swear, I thought I was going crazy—one of the tens was now an eleven! I now had three elevens, two tens and two nines. I think they change according to our energy—I have no doubt that the twelfth hole appeared just for you.

This twelve-hole Abalone has revealed itself to be all about the gift of surprise. The biggest surprise in my life so far has been learning that even when we think we really know ourselves, I—we all—have the capacity to evolve to new levels of awareness. In Abalone terminology, we think we are eleven holes, when overnight we can transform into twelve, thirteen, or beyond. I have evolved from someone certain that I did not sense energy, to one that has learned, through working with the shells, that I have a sensitivity to it. It has taken me some time to share what I've learned because of concerns that it defies logical explanations. But as my insights grow into knowing, there are a few things I would like to teach about shells in connection with energy.

If Abalones connect with our chakras, it would follow that once we reach ten chakras, all paradigms regarding our chakras and our energy dynamics shift. We enter another dimension where energy operates differently. A week after receiving my twelve-hole Abalone, I had an experience that validated this theory. I attended a Spring Equinox ceremony with an energy circle comprising about a dozen people. Just before the ceremony, someone took me aside to ask me about barnacles. I told her about the one shell I have written about previously that is covered with barnacles indicating a loss of identity. However, I was aware that I did not quite have all the information she wanted, so I asked her to let me get back to her. I did not recognize the significance of this conversation at the time, but it foreshadowed the magic awaiting us.

The Equinox celebration was about to begin, and upon entering the sacred space, we were all smudged with sage held in an Abalone shell. For those of you unfamiliar with smudging: it involves sage being lit on fire so that its smoke can purify the energy in its environment.

During this powerful ceremony, a Divinely guided orchestration prepared the way for the main event: a sound-healing CD created by Milagros Phillips entitled *Remember Who You Are*. As Milagros explains, this CD was recorded live and holds the loving intent of awakening the memory of our wholeness. Her voice intoned vibrations that sang our soul's essence. Milagros teaches that "the voice can heal, transform, clear, balance, [and] induce higher states of consciousness as well as still the mind, quiet the body, and bring joy to our environment." As we exited the ceremony, someone drew my attention to the Abalone still holding the smoldering smudge material. *The barnacles on the back of the shell were falling off.* Though I knew that Abalones have been used as smudging vessels countless times, I had never heard of this happening. Those witnessing this Abalone scene became curious about the meaning of this novel occurrence. The person leading the ceremony held my hands and suggested I connect to my twelve-hole Abalone for answers. I heard the word "masks." The barnacles are the masks, or roles we play taking on false identities precisely because we have forgotten who we are. Having a room full of people all intending to step into our truth would cause our masks, or barnacles, to fall away. When we are in our truth, nothing can stick to us that is not real. The smudging Abalone had been exposed to the same powerful healing experience we had, and was either partnering with us, or mirroring what had happened to our energy.

With that in mind, if this new Abalone can shift from eleven holes to twelve holes almost overnight, then perhaps it is reflecting our capacity to quickly shift our energy. At the level of the eleventh chakra, our masks can slip away, and the old rules no longer apply. Consider this: A few years ago it was unheard of to find Abalone with more than seven holes; now they are found with holes numbering in the double digits. A possible explanation for this is beautifully illustrated by a story from the movie *What the *Bleep* Do We Know?* This novel film combines drama, animation, and commentaries by leading scientists that explore the nature of reality.

In the film, we are informed that our brains take in a great deal of information, all of which enters without judgment. This information is then filtered, and it is only to the degree that we are prepared to accept something as "reality" that information enters our conscious awareness. According to *What the Bleep*, we take in 400 billion pieces of information but only 2,000 may reach our awareness. The rest of this information remains unintegrated in our brains, never gaining our attention.

In *What the Bleep*, Columbus' arrival in the New World is dramatized from the viewpoint of the Caribbean Natives. We are told that when the ships first sailed into view, the Natives were not able to see them. This was so foreign to their reality that their conscious awareness was unable to process anything beyond a disturbance on the water. The reenactment focuses upon the shaman who stares out at the ripples in the ocean. With the passage of time, he is suddenly able to see the ships. Once he does, he tells the rest of the tribe. Because of their great trust in this shaman, they see the ships too. The point here is that of course the ships were there all along. The fact that the Natives could not see them did not negate their existence. As the shaman meditated and evolved energetically, he came to a place where his "inner seeing" integrated with his physical eyes, and he finally saw the ships. (By the way, I couldn't help noting that the shaman wears a necklace of Donkey's Ear Abalones, *Haliotis asinina*, six-hole Abalone shells. Kudos to the costume designer—this connects to the third eye chakra, the center for "inner seeing.")

As much as the scientists in this film hope this episode is true, it can never be confirmed since it occurred over five hundred years ago. As I debated whether to include this story in this book, I encountered another demonstration of the mind's ability to filter reality. A friend of mine lives in a nine-member multigenerational family. Her 94-year-old mother-in-law, is quite weak and completely unable to walk without the aid of her walker. In fact, she walks so infrequently that she no longer owns shoes, only slippers. Since her memory is fading, she is often unaware of events that occurred a few hours earlier. Her physical strength is depleted, frequently confining her to bed.

The family keeps a monitor in her room so they can hear if she needs anything. One night, shortly after midnight when she was in bed with a nasty cold, the monitor picked up comments indicating that she had drifted back in time thirty years. She got out of bed and began rummaging through her closet to get dressed. She was frustrated that none of the clothes were hers, and that she couldn't find her shoes. Completely without the aid of her walker, she made her way through the house and began to do housework, with no sign of her cold symptoms. What amazed me about this story is not that her mind could convince her she was living thirty years ago, but that her body would allow her the strength and mobility to follow suit.

The family told me that she can't walk because, although there is nothing physically wrong with her feet, her mind is unable to tell where they are in relation to the ground. Feeling dangerously unsteady, she eventually accepted the fact that she couldn't walk. However, as she revisited her former life, her mind was sending no such message. This is a clear example of the power of the mind to control our reality. Our experiences are based upon our beliefs through conditioning. The next day, her mind returned to current time. Her cold was back in full swing, and she was immobile once again.

If our minds can filter that thoroughly, one can only imagine the worlds surrounding us of which we are not aware—or which some of us are aware, and others call crazy because they are not. As our energy expands, and more information permeates to our conscious awareness, one day we may see these other dimensions. What we must keep in mind is that as easy as it might be to think that they just arrived on the scene, it is more likely that they have been here all along.

What does this have to do with my Abalone shell? Perhaps the Abalone always had twelve or thirteen or more holes and it required my energy to shift in order to see it. If that is the case, then I could shift again and find even more holes in this Abalone shell. The shell is not making new holes; it is my evolution that permits me to see the already existing holes. This is similar to the shift my friend's mother-in-law made from being immobile one day and able to walk the next. The same physical body differed in capabilities due to the information coming from the mind. By the way, some people still see eleven holes in my twelve-hole Abalone.

Years before Abalones entered my life, I entertained similar thoughts after reading *Strangers among Us* by Ruth Montgomery, a book that describes other dimensions as places with different energetic vibration. As she noted, "We see the blades of a fan when it is operated at half speed, but look directly through them when it runs at full speed." In other words, if we could synchronize our energy to theirs by slowing their energy down, or speeding our own up, we would see these other dimensions. I wrote a little poem about this called "Blades from Another Dimension":

Look at a fan before it is turned on
See the blades outlined nice and clear
Switch it on, increase the speed, and you're looking at a blur
The blades seem to completely disappear.

And yet you know those blades are still there
You can prove it by slowing down the speed.
You'll feel a change in the movement of the air
A speed control knob—that is all you need.

Now imagine a fan already spinning fast
With no obvious way for you the speed to tame.
Its blades are still there, just a blur as they pass
You do not see them, but they are there just the same.

Other dimensions are like the blades of this last fan
Vibrating too quickly for us to see
Yet though many can not see them—others can
They have found a way to control the speed.

The blades of the fan are turning slower now for me
A whole new world is opening up before my eyes.
I am just experiencing now what was always there to see
And believe me, it really took me by surprise.

There are auras, like halos, surrounding everyone I know
Around objects and plants they seem to cling.
They dance around buildings, a spectacular light show
Now that I see them, I don't want to miss a thing.

I don't know what I've done to make the blades slow down
Revealing new wonders every day.
Because there is no reason I can consciously point to
I awake each day afraid they've gone away.

Then I look out my window and see a skyline of pure light
Such a comforting feeling washes over me.
Concern is replaced by excitement at the thought of what new sight
Might appear from this "hidden" galaxy.

Twenty years later, I realize that I may have had this reversed. Rather than the blades from other dimensions slowing down, the synchronization may be due to my own energy undergoing alterations. As our vibrations accelerate, allowing us to venture into new domains, speculation remains that we would become invisible to those still vibrating at the current speed. This is the case presented in the *Celestine Prophecy* by James Redfield. I have no idea where connecting to these new dimensions will lead, but I would like to speak about one more shell that could prove to be of great importance.

Indigo Energy
Bednall's Volute (*Volutoconus bednalli*: front cover, photo 35)
This lesson in energy intensified when I had the pleasure of viewing the independent movie *Indigo*. The opening scene shows childhood drawings of something resembling a spider's web or a huge net, an image that triggered a memory in me that I had had fifteen years earlier, when I used to see a net made of light encompassing the entire sky. At first a curiosity, over many months this energy net evolved into something akin to a familiar friend.

In *Indigo* the movie, to my immense satisfaction, the mystery of this energy network was solved. The children refer to it as "the grid" and this is how they visit each other without physically being in each other's presence.

I felt a similar emotion when I saw my first photograph of a Bednalli Volute shell (see the front cover, photo 35): a creamy shell exterior covered with a dark brown cobweb pattern. This too reminded me of my old friend, the energy network in the sky. Every new shell book would open randomly upon a picture of this shell, which I finally decided might be a sign to get my own. It was one of the last shells I bought before completing my last book, and though I am pleased I was able to introduce it to others, I played it safe, barely suggesting the energy network. I described the shell as meaning "networking and connections." I included this note: "Networking involves partnering with others. Together, these connections form a whole that is greater than the sum of its parts. This shell refers to connections on many levels. It is about reaching out to others, joining forces, and discovering that even seemingly unrelated or distant things are connected."

After watching *Indigo*, I feel such wonder at the possibilities represented by this energy network. While I search for confirmation, seeking to completely trust the knowing, ironically, the *Indigo* movie informs us that Indigo children lack self-doubt. They know what they know and there is no talking themselves out of things. Looking back, I realize that I encountered one of these incredible children many years ago, when I was invited to be part of a group of psychic readers visiting a private high school. At the time, my method for shell reading was to travel with a huge wooden display case containing trays holding photographs of three hundred different shells. I love working with children but I was not prepared for the last teenager of the night. He sat down before the display, selected some shells and arranged them. Before I began the interpretation, he suddenly asked if there was a shell that meant depression. I was about to reply, when he closed his eyes and said, "Oh, it's purple." He then opened his eyes, looked back at the three hundred shells before him, and immediately pointed to the Purple Drupe stating, "That one."

I was completely flabbergasted, but, trying to remain professional, I reached down to take out the list of all the shells in the display. I had never shown this list to anyone before, but I told him that he had just pointed to the Purple Drupe and to please note its definition, which, in fact, is "depression, may require counseling." Unlike me, he took this insight in stride as if we were stating the obvious—what was the big deal? Instead, he inquired if I could tell what his biggest fear was. He then pointed to a yellow cone shell. I explained that the cone shell meant cowardice that leads to missed opportunities. He digested that, and then asked me if I thought he would have to leave school. Finally, I looked at the shells he had selected for his reading, and saw that the Papyrus scallop, the shell for school or study, was in a prominent placement. So was the Saul's Murex, the shell for a therapist. His arrangement clearly indicated he was already in therapy regarding an issue involving school.

As the reading continued, I discovered that he had two siblings who were able to read a textbook, retain the information, and get terrific grades. He, on the other hand, had a learning disability. It was nearly impossible for him to read a textbook. Undaunted, he was determined to be like his brother and sister, and expended every ounce of energy he had in an effort to read a book and get equally good grades. His health was deteriorating as a result, and his teachers, parents, and therapist were all suggesting he leave the school. After reading his shells it became quite evident that he would rather die than leave the school. I asked him if anyone knew how strongly he felt about remaining in school. His reply was to point to the shell that meant "to thine own self be true" and tell me, "They don't know. I don't want them to know me." My heart broke at this revelation. This young man had clearly demonstrated to me that he already spoke the language of seashells. My appreciation for his knowledge was dwarfed by the sad recognition that he had all kinds of information inside him that would never be developed as long as he yearned to mimic his siblings.

I was so immersed in these thoughts that I was startled when someone approached us to say that he had to get back to his room immediately to make his dorm's curfew. He hurried off, and only then did I realize that I was alone. Apparently all the other children and readers had left much earlier. Unfortunately, in his haste to get back to his room, I never got his name, and he never got any of my contact information. For months, my greatest wish was for someone to help him realize that leaving school was not running away from something, but running toward something greater. I have come to believe that seeds were planted that night. I will be forever grateful to him. Although he didn't seem to recognize the significance of the volumes of information residing inside him, I felt his knowledge of the shells validated the writing of my first book.

I later met another young woman who was easily able to connect to shell wisdom. Luci attended a two-day shell divination workshop where I had over fifty shells displayed on a table. Upon seeing certain shells, she referred to them by name. I questioned her as to how she knew so much, and she said she bought my previous book a week earlier. Still, it would require a photographic memory to be so accurate. Then she looked at other shells displayed on the table and admired the "mermaid's comb," as she called it. That information was not in my first book—she was quoting from *this* book, *Ocean Wisdom*, which was still in manuscript form tucked in my briefcase. With a wonderful sense of déjà-vu, I removed the spiral-bound manuscript and turned to the section on the Venus Comb Murex revealing that she already knew its contents. Many clients have likened this shell's spines to that of a fish skeleton, but in twenty years of shell reading, nobody had ever called it a mermaid's comb. Yet, as you have read earlier in this book, this was precisely what the man who named it envisioned. While I marveled at her insight, before the workshop ended, her eyes fell upon some Unicorn Horn shells I have not yet written about. When she mentioned their name and meaning I was in awe. Once again, I removed the spiral bound manuscript. Tucked in the back were some loose pages with new information for a third book I am planning on shell energy. I showed her the section on Unicorn Horns where she had quoted the information. It was obvious to me that like the high school boy, she was already connected to the wisdom I was discovering and sharing through my books.

She not only intuited the meaning of the Bednalli Volute shell (there is some information about this shell in the book she possessed, though she hadn't read it yet), but she also showed up at the next class with an Abalone shell and told me that she always wondered about the animals that made them and what the holes were for. I usually reserve the Abalone energy information for the end of the workshop, but she was clearly on an accelerated path. Unlike the high school boy, who had acted unfazed, she wondered at how she knew this information.

There is one other piece to Luci's story. She informed me that she had never been drawn to tarot decks before, but she bought *Ocean Oracle* because her father was an ocean person. At the end of the workshop, I have the students perform their own readings. The first shell Luci selected was the shell about depression. She revealed that, although she is basically an upbeat person, sometimes she goes into very deep depressions. She had no idea why she visited these dark places. Luci also selected the shell for "father" and placed it next to "heart problems." When I saw this, I asked her if her father was still alive. She told me he died from a heart attack when she was a teenager. Next to these shells, she had placed the shell for "forgiveness." This prompted me to ask her if she blamed him for dying? Tears rolled down her cheeks, which surprised her because she had never grieved. She placed her hand over her heart, and told me that she was afraid that he had left her "in here." Then she told me that there were rumors that he had taken antidepressants. This brought everything together. The reason she visited the dark places was because she feared that he had left her, and by visiting his world she could keep him with her. However, as she saw in this reading, he was right by her side, communicating through the shells. Her face lit up as she discovered that she could communicate with him in healthy ways rather than going into darkness. She planned to take the deck to his grave to connect with him. I suggested that since she was obviously on the grid, she could learn to communicate directly. She left the workshop completely transformed by this revelation. Although she began the workshop not quite ready to fully embrace energy work, she left eager to explore what other gifts she possessed.

I assume there are other people—often children—with similar connections to shells, and I hope they avail themselves of this tool for personal growth. I always suspected that being "psychic" is just some people's ability to perceive or receive information that we all broadcast in our energy. We tend to treat intuitives as privileged people with special abilities, but I believe one day reading energy will be the norm. Interacting with the first boy, I was given a taste of what the world will be like when connection to Universal energy is the norm: we just know what we know.

Since I had more resistance to this knowing than these young people I encountered, it took me longer to release my conditioned doubts, but the shells have patiently led me on a steady journey to what promises to be an unlimited source of joyful insight and connection. My twelve-hole Abalone assisted me in connecting with the knowing, making me aware of the Bednalli Volute. This is a costly shell, but fortunately photographs still allow connection to this energy too. If you desire, you or your child can use the shell on the front cover to connect with the grid and Indigo energy.

Journey Back to Your True Path

Before closing *Ocean Wisdom*, I would like to offer an opportunity to journey to a new level of conscious awareness assisted by various light beings visiting from the sea. Please recognize that your life has been perfectly lived until now. Do you feel challenged by this suggestion? Perhaps you recall discomforting events that have been locked away inside you, experiences for which you can find no positive purpose and have relegated to an unceremonious burial. Your shell guides today will be your companions to bring honor to the parts of you that were unsafe to expose. They will reveal information enabling you to shift consciousness. Every life lesson, every experience has value. They have culminated in this moment: providing the foundation for your journey today. Your travels will take you to each of your major energy centers to retrieve parts of yourself you have blocked or hidden away. Uncovering and integrating each piece, will allow you to emerge a more powerfully aligned spiritual being.

To begin, please take a moment to acquaint yourself with all the guides here to assist you in this process. Their images can be found on the back cover. You will be meeting each in sequence beginning with the Tiger Cowrie (top, photo 8 and bottom, photo 9). Next, greet the Starfish (photo 1), Golden Cowrie (photo 2), Giant Pacific Cockle (photo 3), Heart Cockle (photo 4), Pencil Urchin (photo 5), Purple Top Cowrie (photo 6), and Sand Dollar (photo 7). They look forward to working with you in joyous anticipation.

Permit yourself ample opportunity to become familiar with these guides from the earlier notes on Tiger Cowrie (page 7), Starfish (page 2), and Sand Dollar (page 3), and from the following:

Golden Cowrie
Once extremely rare, Golden Cowries were found in Fiji, and only the chiefs were allowed to have them. The Fijian culture believed the Cowrie shell housed the souls of their possessors, and to protect this precious cargo, the chiefs would place a curse upon their shell. Because of this historic connection to a curse, the Golden Cowrie, can communicate a feeling of bad luck, a consequence of selling your soul in pursuit of pleasure.

Giant Pacific Cockle
Anatomically, Cockles possess very powerful foot muscles—enough strength to allow the mollusk to jump. In divination, Cockles connect to jumping themes. The Giant Pacific Cockle is about someone who is very demanding, who expects you to jump through hoops. Inevitably, the person attracted to this shell is more demanding upon himself than anyone else could be.

Heart Cockle
Heart Cockles are associated with love and romance. Because of their appearance, sailors used these shells as valentines for their sweethearts.

Pencil Urchin
The name "pencil" refers to the resemblance of the urchin's spines to writing implements. This connects the Pencil Urchin to the theme of communication. Interestingly, the scientific name for any Urchin without its spines is a "test." When this Urchin appears, it indicates a test of someone's communication skills.

Purple Top Cowrie
Because of their resemblance to human eyes, in ancient Egypt, Cowries were placed in the eye sockets of mummies to give them vision in the afterlife. Consequently, working with this shell involves seeing into other dimensions.

Guided Meditation

Now let's proceed: Find a place where you can get comfortable, seated or laying down. Give yourself plenty of space to stretch out. Ground and center yourself. Take a deep breath, and as you exhale feel yourself becoming more and more relaxed. Again, inhale…exhale…let go.

In your mind's eye, see yourself on a glorious beach of white sand. A warm breeze brushes your face and carries the taste of salt from the clear blue ocean close by. Listen to the sound of the waves gently lapping the shore. The rhythm of the ocean is accompanied by harmonizing calls from the gulls. Feel the sand beneath your bare feet and note the perfect temperature. The smooth grains are toasty warm without burning your skin. Allow the warmth from the sun overhead and the sand beneath you to infiltrate your entire body. Your muscles gladly release all tension. Wiggle your toes in the sand and notice how limber they have become. As the warmth proceeds to penetrate every cell in your body you become completely relaxed. The comforting heat spreads up your legs, torso, and arms. It gently soothes your furrowed brow and encourages you to unclench your jaw and rotate the loosened muscles in your neck. Take a moment to bask in this natural sauna, allowing a sigh of pleasure to escape from your lips.

In this tranquil state, begin strolling toward the ocean. As you approach the water's edge, at your feet you encounter a Tiger Cowrie. Reach down and pick up the Cowrie and run your fingers over its glossy surface. As you turn the shell over you see the puckered slit running along the underside of the shell. The Cowrie you now hold is the womb for today's birth into a new level of awareness. It provides a safe, nurturing energy for you to undertake this growth process with faith in the outcome.

The journey now leads into the ocean where your shell guides will join you one by one. If at any time, you prefer to remain in your current location, know that your guides will be carried by the ocean currents and delivered to you. At all times, they wish you to experience this journey the way that feels most comfortable to you. On the walk out to sea, they are your companions to point out discoveries for your observation. On the journey back to shore, they will assist in retrieving and integrating the pieces you find. Throughout your travels, Tiger Cowrie maintains its nurturing womb embracing you as you grow.

When you are ready, begin a leisurely stroll into the crystal clear ocean to meet your next guide. The sun's rays have warmed the water, drawing you a welcoming bath. Continue walking, allowing the water to rise past your knees and thighs, until it reaches the level of your spine. As you pause here to take in this beautiful vista, you notice a Starfish. Starfish is here to assist you in discovering what behaviors you might have performed that disgusted you, or turned your stomach. With Starfish pointing the way, you can see that at the time, you believed these actions to be necessary for survival in the material world. Ask yourself where you might have abandoned your spiritual pursuits in order to meet survival needs. Starfish reaches out in companionship to hold your hand. As Starfish reaches out to you, if you notice any resistance, simply notice without judgment and choose to walk through it. It is safe to expose these dark places so you can heal and release them. There is no shame today. These are simply lessons, choices you made related to the material world. Spend some time with Starfish as you pry open the places where you have stored your hidden disgust.

Walk in a little farther now, until the water is a few inches below your navel at your hips. Looking around, you spot a creamy orange Golden Cowrie, the shell Fiji chieftains believed housed their soul. You have arrived at the energy center associated with sexual and other pleasures. Perhaps Golden Cowrie is here to aid you in discovering where your soul was stolen in pursuit of pleasure. Where did you leave your truth behind when tempted by desires? Or is Golden Cowrie here to show you how you have denied yourself pleasures? Did you not think you were deserving? Have you been disconnected from your body? This center is the seat of creativity and being open to healthy pleasures allows creative energy to flow. Spend a while with Golden Cowrie delving into the secret parts of you to ponder these questions.

Now walk in a few more steps and feel the water surround your navel. As you pause once again, with your arms dangling at your side, a Giant Pacific Cockle finds its way into your palm. This Cockle, with its strong power to jump, is here at the energy center concerning your ego and self-image. As your companion, it asks you to consider what hoops you jumped through to bolster your self-esteem? What pieces did you force yourself to hide thinking you wouldn't be accepted if this portion of your truth were exposed? Spend time with this yellow Cockle to reveal what demands you placed upon yourself that hid your true identity.

Take several more steps until the water caresses your heart. Look down upon the water to discover a perfect Heart Cockle, the energy center associated with love and relationships. Heart Cockle is your guide to determine where you strayed from your path in pursuit of love. Spend time with this compassionate guide to learn what pieces of yourself were locked away in order to remain in relationships.

Now, venture in a little deeper until the water tickles your throat. It is time to meet Pencil Urchin here at the energy center for communication. Written or spoken, take a little time to explore where you failed to express your truth. Remember your guides will be along later to assist you with whatever you discover.

As you continue walking, you become one with the water. It surrounds you like liquid air, and you find yourself breathing effortlessly. The water is now at your forehead. A Purple Top Cowrie appears. This shell is connected to your spiritual eyes and ears beyond the level of your physical senses. The Purple Top Cowrie guides you to discover where you denied your gut instinct in favor of trusting your eyes and ears. If you allow it, your intuition can assist you in recognizing truths beyond what your physical senses can detect. With this Cowrie by your side, revelations here concern where you might have sabotaged your relationship with your intuitive self and blocked your inner wisdom.

Finally, walk out until you are completely immersed in the water. With the water covering you, you have arrived at the energy center connected to your Divinity and spirituality. Your guide at this realm is Sand Dollar. If we can see a reflection of Divinity in this Sand Dollar, certainly this Divinity must exist in us too. Sand Dollar whispers the question: where did you feel abandoned by God? Angry with God? What might have compelled you to block your connection to Divine energy? Review the choices you made that separated you from this connection.

Now, holding Sand Dollar above your head, allow Sand Dollar to assist you in strengthening your connection to God. Feel the energy begin to enter from above your head reconnecting you to your Divine self. Enjoy the comfort and empowerment you feel radiating with this energy in full partnership with your Divinity.

You are now ready to begin your walk back to shore. When you feel the air on your forehead, rest a moment. Holding the Purple Top Cowrie to your forehead, permit the energy from above to travel down to your forehead and clear the channels to your third eye. Allow your intuition to serve you fully.

Continue walking until your entire head emerges and the water surrounds your throat. Hold the Pencil Urchin against your throat and feel it aid you in clearing the energy blockages that prevented you from speaking your truth.

Now work your way closer to shore until the water level reaches your heart. Hold the Heart Cockle against your chest and feel the energy move from your throat to your heart. Allow it to penetrate through the layers composed of who you were told you were supposed to be, and who you attempted to become in pursuit of love. Let the energy shine upon the truth written deep in your heart. Bathe in your beauty as your loving heart is washed clean.

Continue on your journey toward shore. As you hold the Giant Pacific Cockle near your navel, feel the energy coarse through your body. What demands did you place upon yourself that no longer serve you? Allow the Cockle to assist in dissolving the hold these demands had upon you separating you from acting in your truth.

As you get closer to shore, with the water at your hips, reach down and place the Golden Cowrie against your body. Allow the energy to flow to your hips and assist you in understanding why previous pleasurable pursuits were unfulfilling or denied. The Cowrie encourages discernment for it knows lasting pleasure comes from the desires of your soul, not the shallow desires of your personality. Allow time for the Cowrie to partner with you in dissolving the cords derived from your personality, and to fasten new cords that connect your desires directly to your soul.

On your last stop before returning to the beach, the water is circling you at the base of your spine. Feel the energy stretch down your spine as you hold the Starfish against you at the water's surface. Wherever you find yourself disgusted with choices you made for survival, Starfish is here to offer its strength for you to choose again, to survive without compromising your truth.

The energy now flows easily through your entire body. You are vibrant and healthy, radiant in your truth. Your guides are rejoicing and their contagious celebration has spread to other creatures in the sea. Dolphins are dancing and whales are singing—come join this festival in your honor!

As you depart from this scene, know that there may be other truths you need to discover in the future. We are in a constant state of growth and expansion. Know that you can return to this beach anytime you wish, and your guides will be waiting to join you on your next journey.

As you return to shore, no longer buoyed by the water, you become aware of your body's weight once again. Walking up the beach, surrounded by the sun's warm rays, you feel the drops of ocean water evaporating from your skin. The toasty warmth makes quick work of drying you thoroughly. As you say a temporary good-bye, it is time to return to your surroundings. Begin to feel the physical sensations as you move back into your body. Stretch out your arms and legs and rotate your head from side to side. Know that during your journey, you made wonderful choices for yourself. Slowly open your eyes. You are returning alert, relaxed, and joyful in the knowledge that you have reached a new level of spiritual growth.

Conversion Chart for *Ocean Oracle*

Keeping in mind that shell cards contain the energy of the shells, you are invited to apply the information in this book to the shell card deck in *Ocean Oracle*. Should you wish to do so, here is a chart converting the shell numbers in *Ocean Wisdom* to their respective numbers in the *Ocean Oracle* deck.

COMMON NAME	SCIENTIFIC NAME	SHELL NUMBER IN *OCEAN WISDOM*	SHELL NUBMER IN *OCEAN ORACLE*
Starfish		1	58
Golden Cowrie	*Cypraea aurantium*	2	81
Giant Pacific Cockle	*Laevicardium elatum*	3	9
Heart Cockle	*Corculum cardissa*	4	73
Pencil Urchin	*Heterocentrotus mammillatus*	5	163
Sand Dollar	*Mellita quinquiesperforata*	7	95
Tiger Cowire	*Cypraea tigris*	8/9	85
Razor Clam	*Ensis siliqua*	10	94
Delicate File Clam (Giant	*Acesta phillipinensis*	11	26
Purpura Murex	*Bolinus brandaris*	12	89
Wide-Mouthed Purpura	*Purpura patula*	13	93
St. James Scallop	*Pecten maximus*	14	96
Worm Shell	*Vermicularia spirata*	16	65
Miller's Nutmeg	*Trigonostoma milleri*	17	40
Moon Snail	*Neverita duplicata*	18	31
Suttlecock Volva	*Volva volva*	19	167
Mussel	*Mytilus edulis*	20	33
Venus Comb Murex	*Murex pecten*	21	150
Land Snail	*Placostylus*	22	55
Janthina	*Janthina janthina*	23	23
Harp Shell	*Harpa ventricosa*	24	20
Textile Cone Shell	*Conus textile*	25	80
Geography Cone Shell	*Conus geographus*	26	76
Tropidophora Land Snail	*Tropidophora deliciosa*	28	190
Sea Biscuit	*Clypeaster rosaceus*	29	187
Fossil Cephalopod		30	174
Long Spined Star Shell	*Astraea phoebia*	31	193
Pink Conch	*Strombus gigas*	32	74
Nigrite Murex	*Hexaplex nigritus*	33	178
Helmet Conch	*Cassis tuberosa*	34	22
Bednalli Volute	*Volutoconus bednalli*	35	199
* Purple Top Cowrie	*Cypraea caputserpentis*	6	
Idol's Eye Cowrie	*Cypraea asellus*		82

* Both the Purple Top Cowrie in Ocean Wisdom, and Idol's Eye Cowrie in *Ocean Oracle* connect to the third eye, or 6th chakra.

References

Allen, Casslyn. Symphonies of the Heart energetics consulting. www.symphoniesoftheheart.com

Casarjian, Robin. *Houses of Healing: A Prisoner's Guide to Inner Power and Freedom.* Boston:The Lionheart Foundation, 1995.

Coleman, Neville. *Shells Alive!* London: Rigby Publishers Limited, 1981.

Emoto, Masuro. [trans. David A.Thayne]. *The Hidden Messages in Water.* Hillsboro, OR: Beyond Words Publishing, Inc., 2004.

Foundation for Inner Peace. *A Course in Miracles.* New York: Viking Adult, (2nd ed.), 1996.

Fountain, Henry. "Snails, Desired for Beauty and Venom, May Be Threatened." *New York Times*, 21 October 2003.

Gordon, N.R.. *Seashells, Treasures from the Sea.* New York: Friedman/Fairfax Publishers, 1994.

Hanson, Michelle. *Ocean Oracle: What Seashells Reveal About Our True Nature*, Hillsboro, OR: Beyond Words Publishing, Inc., 2004.

Launius, Roger D. "Octave Chanute: The Chicago Connection and the Birth of Aviation," Illinois Periodicals Online/Aviation. www.lib.niu.edu/ipo/2001/iht810114.html.

Kalb, Claudia. "Pharmacy Island." *Newsweek (Special Edition: The Future of Medicine)*, 2005, 55–8.

Millman, Dan. *Way of the Peaceful Warrior.* Tiburon, CA: H.J.Kramer, Inc., 1980.

Montgomery, Ruth. *Strangers Among Us.* New York: Fawcett Crest Books, 1979.

Northrup, Christiane. www.drnorthrup.com.

Phillips, Milagros. *"Remember Who You Are!",* Soaring Sounds Productions. www.thesoundof light.com.

Redfield, James. *The Celestine Prophecy.* Warner Books, Inc., 1993.

Rumi, Jalal-al-Din. [trans. Coleman Barks]. *The Essential Rumi.* San Francisco: Harper, 1997.

Shell Group, The. "100 Years of the Pecten: The History of the Shell Emblem." www.shell.com.

Spiritual Cinema Circle. *Indigo.* 2005.

Tanner, Lindsay. "Synthetic snail venom might relieve cancer pain." *Associated Press,* 6 January 2004.

Wilson, Steve. Shaman's Song energy healing, and Soaring Sounds Productions. ste9wil@aol.com